I0410807

PORT OF ENTRY INFRASTRUCTURE: HOW DOES THE FEDERAL GOVERNMENT PRIORITIZE INVESTMENTS?

HEARING

BEFORE THE

SUBCOMMITTEE ON BORDER AND MARITIME SECURITY

OF THE

COMMITTEE ON HOMELAND SECURITY HOUSE OF REPRESENTATIVES

ONE HUNDRED THIRTEENTH CONGRESS

SECOND SESSION

JULY 16, 2014

Serial No. 113–78

Printed for the use of the Committee on Homeland Security

Available via the World Wide Web: http://www.gpo.gov/fdsys/

U.S. GOVERNMENT PRINTING OFFICE

91–930 PDF   WASHINGTON : 2015

For sale by the Superintendent of Documents, U.S. Government Printing Office
Internet: bookstore.gpo.gov   Phone: toll free (866) 512–1800; DC area (202) 512–1800
Fax: (202) 512–2250   Mail: Stop SSOP, Washington, DC 20402–0001

COMMITTEE ON HOMELAND SECURITY

MICHAEL T. MCCAUL, Texas, *Chairman*

LAMAR SMITH, Texas
PETER T. KING, New York
MIKE ROGERS, Alabama
PAUL C. BROUN, Georgia
CANDICE S. MILLER, Michigan, *Vice Chair*
PATRICK MEEHAN, Pennsylvania
JEFF DUNCAN, South Carolina
TOM MARINO, Pennsylvania
JASON CHAFFETZ, Utah
STEVEN M. PALAZZO, Mississippi
LOU BARLETTA, Pennsylvania
RICHARD HUDSON, North Carolina
STEVE DAINES, Montana
SUSAN W. BROOKS, Indiana
SCOTT PERRY, Pennsylvania
MARK SANFORD, South Carolina
CURTIS CLAWSON, Florida

BENNIE G. THOMPSON, Mississippi
LORETTA SANCHEZ, California
SHEILA JACKSON LEE, Texas
YVETTE D. CLARKE, New York
BRIAN HIGGINS, New York
CEDRIC L. RICHMOND, Louisiana
WILLIAM R. KEATING, Massachusetts
RON BARBER, Arizona
DONDALD M. PAYNE, JR., New Jersey
BETO O'ROURKE, Texas
FILEMON VELA, Texas
ERIC SWALWELL, California
VACANCY
VACANCY

BRENDAN P. SHIELDS, *Staff Director*
JOAN O'HARA, *Acting Chief Counsel*
MICHAEL S. TWINCHEK, *Chief Clerk*
I. LANIER AVANT, *Minority Staff Director*

————

SUBCOMMITTEE ON BORDER AND MARITIME SECURITY

CANDICE S. MILLER, Michigan, *Chairwoman*

JEFF DUNCAN, South Carolina
TOM MARINO, Pennsylvania
STEVEN M. PALAZZO, Mississippi
LOU BARLETTA, Pennsylvania
CURTIS CLAWSON, Florida
MICHAEL T. MCCAUL, Texas *(Ex Officio)*

SHEILA JACKSON LEE, Texas
LORETTA SANCHEZ, California
BETO O'ROURKE, Texas
VACANCY
BENNIE G. THOMPSON, Mississippi *(Ex Officio)*

PAUL L. ANSTINE, II, *Subcommittee Staff Director*
DEBORAH JORDAN, *Subcommittee Clerk*
ALISON NORTHROP, *Minority Subcommittee Staff Director*

CONTENTS

PORT OF ENTRY INFRASTRUCTURE: HOW DOES THE FEDERAL GOVERNMENT PRIORITIZE INVESTMENTS?

Wednesday, July 16, 2014

U.S. HOUSE OF REPRESENTATIVES,
SUBCOMMITTEE ON BORDER AND MARITIME SECURITY,
COMMITTEE ON HOMELAND SECURITY,
Washington, DC.

The subcommittee met, pursuant to call, at 10:02 a.m., in Room 311, Cannon House Office Building, Hon. Candice S. Miller [Chairwoman of the subcommittee] presiding.

Present: Representatives Miller, Duncan, Marino, Barletta, Clawson, Jackson Lee, and O'Rourke.

Also present: Representative Keating.

Mrs. MILLER. Appreciate the witnesses taking their seats there. Both Mr. Marino and I actually have mark-ups in other committees this morning, so we are going to try to start right here on time.

The Committee on Homeland Security, the Subcommittee on Border and Maritime Security will come to order. The subcommittee is meeting today to examine ports of entry infrastructure investment priorities, and we are certainly pleased today to be joined by Mr. John Wagner, of the U.S. Customs and Border Protection, who is accompanied by Mr. Eugene Schied—also CBP; and Mr. Michael Gelber, of the General Services Administration; and Mr. Oscar Leeser, who is the mayor of El Paso.

Mr. Mayor, thank you very, very much for attending today. We certainly appreciate you traveling to Washington to join with us today.

Our Nation relies on the efficient flow of commerce across our border, and it is the job of the U.S. Customs and Border Protection to not only facilitate commerce, but to also secure the homeland. To accomplish this mission, sufficient port of entry infrastructure is needed along with robust Customs and Border Protection staffing.

CBP's important mission not only keeps America safe, but also ensures tens of thousands of American jobs and billions of dollars in commerce that come into our country through trade with Canada and with Mexico.

A significant portion of the trade with Canada, our No. 1 trading partner—actually our Nation's No. 1 trading partner—and Mexico, who is our Nation's No. 2 trading partner, cross nearly 170 land ports of entry every day. It goes without saying that delays and backups caused by old and inadequate infrastructure cost businesses millions of dollars in lost opportunities.

This is especially true with just-in-time manufacturing, critical to the auto industry, actually, in my home State of Michigan, so I am very familiar with that. With this being the case, quick cross-border movement is essential. Simply put, if auto parts don't make it across the border in a timely fashion, production lines can actually shut down.

As our economy and security requirements grow, our ports of entry must be able to accommodate more trucks, more passengers and cargo, while at the same time allowing people who cross the border each day convenient and secure travel, as well.

How CBP and the Federal Government as a whole prioritize the need to expand and to update existing ports while also planning for new ports is neither clear nor transparent, and I hope today's hearing will help us all understand this process clearly. While several land ports of entry projects were included in the President's most recent budget request, this committee had not been provided significant information on CBP's strategic plan for port of entry modernization and construction for future projects.

This committee has asked repeatedly for a list of CBP's port of entry priorities, but thus far CBP had been unwilling to share that list with the committee, although I will note that just about 10 minutes ago we received a 4-year-old list, which I have over here, I am going to try to digest a bit.

Many Members of this committee, myself included, have ports of entries in their districts, many of which need improvements. We would like to know where on the list these projects fall, and more importantly, how CBP determines how these projects rank, what the criteria is that they used. Surely that is something that CBP should and can defend to the membership of this committee.

In my own district we have the Blue Water Bridge Plaza expansion, a project that has been in the planning stages actually for more than a decade. The city of Port Huron and the State of Michigan have worked tirelessly to meet the design and the planning demands of CBP through the process, which CBP has changed several times.

Actually, about 150 homes and businesses in the proposed expansion site have already been condemned; they have been demolished to allow for a plaza to meet the needs of CBP. This destruction was based on a promise to build this needed plaza that has not been fulfilled as of yet. Actually, there are almost 60 acres of tax base that has been removed from the city and the county's tax rolls, putting great stress on a community that has been under further stress, of course, of a difficult economy.

Our Canadian partners have actually done their thing. They have expanded their customs plaza on their side of the Blue Water Bridge, actually years ago, with the understanding that the American side of the bridge would also have a plaza upgrade.

So we are shovel-ready, I suppose you could say, in Port Huron, but the funding never seems to come through. City and State leaders have worked with CBP and the Michigan Department of Transportation to revise the plan in an effort to reduce the cost.

I mentioned the Blue Water Bridge. In full transparency, obviously I represent that area. But it is the second-busiest border crossing on the northern tier of our Nation, so it is not just some small crossing. It is an enormous twinned bridge there. Certainly, I think, you know, we should be certainly one of the projects that should be at the head of the line in the Northern Border for ports of entry.

It is not an artist rendering; it is not a proposed crossing. Some that are being considered are, you know, in the design phases, or their—wherever they are in the engineer's drawings, but this is a project that actually exists—a bridge that actually exists, looking for a plaza.

Certainly there are other ports of entry also waiting. But again, there has been no guidance from CBP on how to move forward with the project in my district or in so many other districts across the Nation.

I am certainly mindful, as we all are, of the very tough budget times that we are in. As a Nation we need to make tough choices when it comes to the limited dollars available for ports of entry construction. But the crossing of goods and services across the border helps to grow our economy and our tax base across our Nation—on the Northern Border, on the Southern Border.

It is not frivolous spending. It helps investment in our future economic growth and prosperity, which also would help to add money to the treasury and help ease our budget problems. That is why I fully support, as well, concepts like P3s, or public-private partnerships, as they are called, and other innovative ways to fund infrastructure improvements.

We actually have made a proposal to my Governor in Michigan to consider the Blue Water Bridge Plaza as a P3, and I want to—I will be asking some questions about that. I hope that is something that CBP and GSA can discuss today. Again, I use that as an example. There are plenty of other ports of entry that may be also under consideration for a P3 or some creative financing.

The goal of this hearing today is to really understand CBP's criteria. What is the criteria on their list? How do they prioritize land ports of entry for infrastructure improvements? And to determine how they decide to fund projects and, of course, again, explore the role that public-private partnerships and other unique approaches to financing might play in moving that process along.

So I certainly look forward to hearing from the witnesses today on how we can work together, again, which POEs are on the list, what criteria is used to prioritize who gets funded and when. Because the ports of entry across the Nation are in dire need of modernization and expansion, and I believe we need to tap into the expertise of the private sector, as well, and to partner with them to come up with a better, more cost-effective approach to new ports of entry construction.

At this time I would—Chairwoman recognizes the Ranking Member of the subcommittee, the gentlelady from Texas, Ms. Jackson Lee, for any statement that she may have.

Ms. JACKSON LEE. Thank you very much, Madam Chairwoman. Let me first of all thank you for this continuing oversight that has been so very effective dealing with concerns of border security, but also the importance of the need for the infrastructure, personnel, and other aspects that will improve our Nation's ports and inquire of the experts—local municipal leaders along with leaders in DHS and other experts—on this question. It is enormously important.

So I thank you for holding today's hearing examining how the Federal Government prioritizes investments in port of entry infrastructure.

As a Member from a border State, I understand how important appropriate infrastructure and staffing at our ports of entry are to not just border communities, but our Nation as a whole. On an average day about $2 billion in trade crosses our land borders, creating jobs and bolstering the economy in cities and towns across America.

I have had the privilege of serving on this committee for a number of years, and so I have seen the bustling trade on the Canadian border; I have seen it occur on the California border; certainly the Texas border in cities like El Paso and Laredo. This is a vibrant part of our efforts here in North America. In fact, trade just with Mexico supports 6 million jobs in the United States—a lot of those jobs in Houston, Texas.

Meanwhile, our ports of entry are aging and their infrastructure can no longer accommodate the volume of trucks, vehicles, and pedestrians that cross every day, resulting in increasing wait times. These decades-old facilities were not built to accommodate post-9/11 security technology, either.

CBP previously estimated it would need $6 billion over 10 years to modernize existing ports of entry to meet its current security and facilitation missions. Congress failed to provide funding in fiscal years 2011, 2012, and 2013 for port of entry infrastructure, exacerbating the backlog of infrastructure projects.

Meanwhile, staffing shortages continue to be a problem as CBP remains several thousand officers shy of what its staffing model indicated is necessary to properly staff our Nation's ports of entry. As a result, wait times at many ports of entry continue to grow, costing the U.S. economy and American consumers billions.

I asked the mayor of El Paso, Texas, Oscar Leeser, to join us today to speak about what his community is doing in partnership with CBP to reduce wait times and make improvements at three ports of entry in his city. Let me thank the mayor for his presence here and for being a model for what we should be doing but what cities have been doing.

We thank all of the witnesses for their presence.

I would like to take note of your Member of Congress in particular, my colleague from Texas, Representative Beto O'Rourke, who has been a strong advocate on this committee on border issues. We are pleased to have him representing the community.

As well, I will tell you, I am even pleased to have him mention El Paso more times than I mention Houston. So I am going to congratulate him for that and thank him for his great leadership and his commitment to properly sourcing and staffing our ports of entry.

I hope to hear from the mayor about his thoughts on the ways we can work cooperatively to provide the infrastructure and staffing communities like his, as well as how that can translate across

America. I also look forward to hearing from our Federal witnesses about how ports of entry infrastructure needs are prioritized and what we can do to maximize our limited border security dollars in this area.

I thank the witnesses for joining us today.

I would add, as the Chairwoman knows, we spent a lot of days down at the border just a few weeks ago—maybe 10 days ago—addressing questions of ports of entry that also included the question of the surge of unaccompanied children. I could not be in a hearing dealing with border security infrastructure without commenting on that surge and first of all saying to the administration that your response, and your steady response, which most people did not glean from the surge, but the administration had been dealing with this even before 2014 in October 2013. I think it is important that in the hearing that Chairman McCaul and I co-chaired, we both affirm the need for the introduction on the floor of the House and the passage out of the House of H.R. 1417, a bill that Chairwoman and I have worked extensively on.

Lastly, let me say that this country is a country of laws and people. I think in this particular hearing it is important, as well, to emphasize that the laws we have to deal with unaccompanied children are laws that work—some of the laws generated from a lawsuit that the Government lost—and that we can do the good things of this committee, looking for the rebuild of our infrastructure, what many of you will be talking about, at the same time address the humanitarian crisis with the laws that we have, adding to that the reauthorization of the Customs and Border Patrol Agents and H.R. 1417.

But no laws need to be changed to deny children due process, as has been suggested by the HUMANE Act. We can actually work with the Wilberforce bill, as we have done over the decades.

So I thank the Chairwoman for this hearing.

My last point, Madam Chairwoman, is I am in a mark-up in Judiciary that I have to be at, and so I may depart for a moment, hope to be able to return and hope that we will yield to the gentleman from El Paso if I have to leave at some point, if Ms. Sanchez is not here.

Thank you so very much. Thank you, Madam Chairwoman. I yield back.

[The statement of Ranking Member Jackson Lee follows:]

STATEMENT OF RANKING MEMBER SHEILA JACKSON LEE

JULY 16, 2014

I thank Chairwoman Miller for holding today's hearing examining how the Federal Government prioritizes investments in port of entry infrastructure.

As a Member from a border State, I understand how important appropriate infrastructure and staffing at our ports of entry are to not just border communities, but our Nation as a whole.

On an average day, about $2 billion in trade crosses our land borders, creating jobs and bolstering the economy in cities and towns across America.

In fact, trade just with Mexico supports 6 million jobs in the United States.

Meanwhile, our ports of entry are aging and their infrastructure can no longer accommodate the volume of trucks, vehicles, and pedestrians that cross every day, resulting in increasing wait times.

These decades-old facilities were not built to accommodate post-9/11 security technology either.

CBP previously estimated it would need $6 billion over 10 years to modernize existing ports of entry to meet its current security and facilitation missions.

Congress failed to provide funding in fiscal years 2011, 2012, and 2013 for port of entry infrastructure, exacerbating the backlog of infrastructure projects.

Meanwhile, staffing shortages continue to be a problem, as CBP remains several thousand officers shy of what its staffing model indicated is necessary to properly staff our Nation's ports of entry.

As a result, wait times at many ports of entry continue to grow, costing the U.S. economy—and American consumers—billions.

I asked the mayor of El Paso, Texas, Oscar Leeser, to join us today to speak about what his community is doing, in partnership with CBP, to reduce wait times and make improvements at the three ports of entry in his city.

His Member of Congress, my colleague from Texas, Rep. Beto O'Rourke, is a leader on this committee on border issues, and we are pleased to have a representative from his community share first-hand experience about what we must do to properly resource and staff ports of entry.

I hope to hear from Mayor Leeser about his thoughts on ways we can work cooperatively to provide the infrastructure and staffing communities like his need.

I also look forward to hearing from our Federal witnesses about how port of entry infrastructure needs are prioritized and what we can do to maximize our limited border security dollars in this area.

Mrs. MILLER. I thank the gentlelady. I think you and Mr. Marino are both in that mark-up, I believe; and I am in another mark-up, as well, so we will try to move along here today.

But before I formally introduce our witnesses, I certainly wanted to recognize and welcome our newest Member of our Border and Maritime Security Subcommittee here, Mr. Clawson, from Florida.

I think you will find that this is a very, a very busy and active committee. The work is very interesting and certainly impacts, I know, your district and all of our districts and our Nation. So we certainly welcome you and look forward to your participation and involvement with our committee.

Ms. JACKSON LEE. We welcome you. I will just do a little applause. Thank you.

[Laughter.]

Mrs. MILLER. Other Members of the committee are reminded that opening statements might—may be submitted for the record.

[The statement of Ranking Member Thompson follows:]

PREPARED STATEMENT OF RANKING MEMBER BENNIE G. THOMPSON

JULY 16, 2014

On this committee, we are fortunate to have Members who represent districts on our Northern and Southern Borders and know first-hand the importance of having sufficient infrastructure and staffing at our ports of entry.

Today, there are about 21,775 Customs and Border Protection (CBP) Officers staffing 329 air, land, and sea ports, including 167 at the land borders. On an average day, about $2 billion in trade crosses the land borders, along with 350,000 passenger vehicles, 135,000 pedestrians, and 30,000 trucks. Of all goods moved in U.S. international trade, about a third is with Canada and Mexico, and almost 90 percent of that moves by land.

Unfortunately, port of entry infrastructure and staffing has not kept pace with the demands of this robust travel and commerce. While the 2009 stimulus provided sufficient funding to modernize CBP-owned ports of entry, General Services Administration (GSA) ports remain in dire need of modernization and expansion.

Indeed, unmet needs at just our existing land ports total an estimated $6 billion. In recent years, Congress has failed to provide adequate funding to make progress toward addressing these needs. Indeed, in 3 recent years, until last year, Congress did not provide any funding for land ports at all.

As a result, some ports suffer from insufficient or outdated infrastructure that makes it difficult to deploy necessary, modern security technology or to deploy sufficient personnel to move people and goods in a timely manner.

Similarly, while Congress recently appropriated funding to hire an additional 2,000 CBP Officers, the agency remains several thousand officers short of what it needs to properly staff ports of entry and fulfill its security and trade facilitation missions. This staffing shortage often results in increased wait times and long lines at our land borders for the commuters, visitors, and businesses that rely on cross-border travel.

These wait times have a detrimental effect on the American economy. Delays at U.S.-Mexico border crossings alone cost the U.S. economy an estimated $7.8 billion in 2011. Ultimately, these costs are borne by American consumers. Some communities, like El Paso, which owns three ports of entry, have decided to fill this gap by participating in public-private partnership initiatives authorized by Congress.

Under these arrangements, local entities pick up the tab for CBP Officer staffing to close the gap between the staffing the Government provides and what is necessary to keep wait times reasonable.

While this may be a good stop-gap solution, the Federal Government has a responsibility to provide sufficient funding to ensure CBP has the staffing to carry out its border security and trade facilitation missions.

Today, I look forward to hearing from our witnesses about how port of entry infrastructure needs are identified, prioritized, and ultimately funded. Along with support from Congress, ensuring this process works efficiently is essential to ensuring our ports of entry are ready to meet current demands at our borders.

Mrs. MILLER. Again, we have our distinguished witnesses today.

Mr. John Wagner, who is a frequent visitor here to our committee, the assistant commissioner for U.S. Customs and Border Protection Office of Field Operations. He formerly served as executive director of admissibility and passenger programs with responsibility for all traveler admissibility-related policies and programs, including the Trusted Traveler Program and the Electronic System for Travel Authorization, and the Immigration Advisory Program in the Fraudulent Document Analysis Unit.

He is accompanied this morning by Mr. Schied, who is the assistant commissioner for CBP's Office of Administration. Mr. Schied will not be offering testimony but will be available to answer any of our questions, as I understand it.

So we welcome you, as well.

Mr. Michael Gelber is the deputy commissioner for Public Building Service at the U.S. General Services Administration. The Public Building Service is one of the largest public real estate organizations in the world, operating more than 9,000 owned and leased properties across the United States. He began his career there in 1988 and has held positions—several leadership positions, actually, including service in the Northwest and the Great Lakes regions.

Mr. Oscar Leeser is the mayor of El Paso, and is a position that he has held since June 2014. Before becoming mayor, Mr. Leeser held several leadership positions in the automotive business community in El Paso, and he remains active with the El Paso Children's Hospital foundations.

The witnesses' full written statements will appear in the record.

The Chairwoman now recognizes Mr. Wagner for his testimony.

STATEMENT OF JOHN WAGNER, ASSISTANT COMMISSIONER, OFFICE OF FIELD OPERATIONS, CUSTOMS AND BORDER PROTECTION, U.S. DEPARTMENT OF HOMELAND SECURITY, ACCOMPANIED BY EUGENE H. SCHIED, ASSISTANT COMMISSIONER, OFFICE OF ADMINISTRATION, CUSTOMS AND BORDER PROTECTION, U.S. DEPARTMENT OF HOMELAND SECURITY

Mr. WAGNER. Thank you. Good morning.

Chairwoman Miller, Ranking Member Jackson Lee, and Members of the subcommittee, thank you for the opportunity to appear today to discuss U.S. Customs and Border Protection's efforts to modernize land port of entry facilities and operations in support of our mission to secure and facilitate travel and trade to the United States.

Later this month we celebrate the 225th anniversary of the establishment of the Customs Service, its importance to the history of our Nation, and its continued importance today as part of CBP's complex mission.

The Office of Field Operations is CBP's front-line entity responsible for securing and facilitating international trade and travel at our Nation's 329 ports of entry. During 2013 we processed more than 25 million cargo containers and more than 362 million passengers in the land, sea, and air environments, and trade and travel volumes continue to rise. More than half of the Nation's official ports of entry are located along the U.S. land borders with Mexico and Canada, and most were built to support the distinct and independent operations of pre-DHS components, such as the Customs Service; the Animal and Plant Health Inspection Service; and the Immigration and Naturalization Service.

Today CBP's consolidated operations entail state-of-the-art technology and professional law enforcement personnel to process persons and cargo and maintain an efficient stream of cross-border travel and trade. The success of these operations depends heavily on the condition and operational utility of our inspection facilities and the availability of CBP personnel.

Today I would like to discuss CBP's efforts to satisfy infrastructure and personnel demands and meet the challenge of growing volumes of trade and travel. Several land ports of entry were built more than 70 years ago. Even those constructed as recently as 15 years ago require renovation or replacement to meet present-day security standards, enforcement and facilitation technologies, and growing demands for additional processing capacity.

CBP and the General Services Administration use a multi-step process to plan for all land port of entry modernization investments. In close coordination with key Federal, State, and local stakeholders, we conduct a strategic resource assessment to identify individual needs at each facility and a sensitivity analysis to ascertain the relative urgency of the facility needs Nation-wide. We evaluate the impact of environmental, cultural, historic preservation, and land acquisition requirements and consider the likelihood of obtaining funds.

After a thorough assessment, we arrive at a prioritized capital investment plan that is updated annually to ensure that available Federal funding is directed to the areas of the greatest need.

Modern inspection facilities accommodate cross-border traffic more efficiently and integrate advanced technology equipment more effectively, enhancing CBP's security and facilitation operations. Expediting tourism and commerce is vital to our Nation's economic prosperity, and detecting potentially dangerous people and cargo is essential to National security.

CBP supports the modernization of inspection facilities at our land ports. We actively participate in border master planning and work with State and local stakeholders to determine where and what kind of inspection services and facilities are needed.

CBP is committed to supporting our stakeholders' needs. However, it is not efficient to have every port of entry facility provide the same services and equipment. CBP looks closely at each port's activity and we work with State and local government to appropriately match services and equipment to port activities. We do not want facilities, lanes, equipment, or personnel to sit idle.

CBP's coordination with regional transportation groups is vital to the development of alternative innovative ways to maximize resources and efficiency, especially in constrained budget environments. Segregating or rerouting certain traffic to alternative ports optimizes resources and facilities and is an effective way to meet the needs and volume of specific commercial, vehicle, or pedestrian traffic.

Stacking booths increases traffic throughput, and high-low booths can accommodate the processing of either commercial trucks or personal vehicles. These methods provide CBP with valuable flexibility to quickly adapt to changing port conditions or cross-border volume and reduce the overall footprint of facilities.

Due to the budget environment over the past several years, funding for facilities and personnel—both essential operational elements of ports of entry—has been limited. To keep pace with the growth in international trade and travel, we developed a three-part resource optimization strategy that identifies staffing requirements, ensures the efficient use of resources by optimizing business processes, and explores funding strategies to support these increases.

Thanks to the support of Congress, CBP was recently granted additional authorities to enter into public-private partnerships and pursue alternative methods of funding CBP services and financing ports of entry infrastructure projects. Under Section 560 of the Consolidated and Further Continuing Appropriations Act of 2013, CBP received authority allowing the commissioner to enter into no more than five reimbursable service agreements to provide new or enhanced customs and immigration-related inspection services.

We entered into these agreements with the participating locations last December. In the first 6 months of the program CBP was able to provide an additional 7,000 CBP Officer assignments and open primary lanes and booths for an additional 18,000 hours at the request of our partners, increasing border processing throughput at the participating ports of entry.

In 2014 CBP received additional authority under Section 559 of the Consolidated Appropriations Act of 2014, which authorizes us to enter into partnerships with private-sector and Government entities at ports of entry to reimburse certain costs of services and accept donations of real and personal property.

Chairwoman Miller, Ranking Member Jackson Lee, and Members of the subcommittee, thank you for the opportunity to testify today, and I am happy to answer your questions.

[The prepared statement of Mr. Wagner follows:]

Prepared Statement of John Wagner

July 16, 2014

Chairwoman Miller, Ranking Member Jackson Lee, and distinguished Members of the subcommittee, thank you for the opportunity to discuss U.S. Customs and Border Protection's (CBP) efforts to sustain and modernize our Nation's land ports of entry (LPOEs) to secure and facilitate growing volumes of travel and trade.

CBP is responsible for securing the Nation's borders at and between ports of entry (POEs), while facilitating the efficient movement of legitimate travel and trade. Later this month, we celebrate the 225th anniversary of the establishment of the U.S. Customs Service and the important role it played in the history of our Nation. Since its merger into CBP in 2003, Customs has remained a part of CBP's heritage and a significant presence in the continuation of our mission. Today, CBP serves as the front line in defending the American public against terrorists and instruments of terror and protects our economic security while facilitating lawful international travel and trade. CBP takes a comprehensive approach to border management and control, combining National security, customs, immigration, and agricultural protection into a coordinated whole.

The Office of Field Operations (OFO) is the law enforcement entity within CBP responsible for carrying out CBP's complex and demanding mission at all POEs. OFO manages the lawful access to our Nation and economy by securing and facilitating international trade and travel. Staffing challenges at the POEs continue to increase as CBP takes on additional mission requirements and as trade and travel volumes continue to grow. To address this on-going challenge, we have developed a three-part Resource Optimization Strategy that: (1) Identifies staffing requirements using a Workload Staffing Model; (2) ensures the efficient use of resources by optimizing current business processes; and (3) explores funding strategies to support staffing increases.

The Workload Staffing Model employs a rigorous, data-driven methodology to identify staffing requirements by considering all the activities performed by CBP Officers at our POEs, the volume of those activities, and the levels of effort required to carry them out. The most recent results of this model show a need for 4,373 additional CBP Officers through fiscal year 2015.

Thanks to the support of Congress, the *Consolidated Appropriations Act, 2014,* Pub. L. 113–76, included funding for 2,000 new CBP Officers. These additional officers will be allocated utilizing the Workload Staffing Model and directed to those ports with the greatest need. While the 2,000 additional officers will bring significant support to our mission, it is important to note that this is a good down-payment, but unfortunately, no POE will be "made whole" by this allocation of officers. The President's fiscal year 2015 budget request calls for user fee increases that would fund an additional 2,000 CBP Officers. Additionally, CBP will continue to pursue transformation efforts, new reimbursement authorities, and partnerships with our stakeholders.

There are more people and goods coming through our ports of entry than ever before. Since 2009, we have seen growth in both trade and travel and we expect these trends to continue. Every year, OFO facilitates the travel of tens of millions of international tourists visiting our Nation. In fiscal year 2013, CBP inspected more than 360 million travelers at our air, land, and sea POEs. The facilitation and security of lawful travel and trade is a priority for CBP and we are taking steps, working closely with our stakeholders, Congress, and the U.S. General Services Administration (GSA), to improve our POEs and our security and facilitation efforts. At CBP, we view effective and efficient security as a contributor to facilitation, and not a barrier. Security measures are vital to protecting travel and trade from the damaging effects of terrorist or other security incidents. Our goals of National security and economic prosperity are fundamentally intertwined.

CBP's role in securing and facilitating international trade and travel is critical to the growth of our economy and the creation of more jobs. The extent to which wait times affect the local and National economy was most recently studied by the National Center for Risk and Economic Analysis of Terrorism Events (CREATE), a Department of Homeland Security (DHS) Center of Excellence. CREATE issued "The Impact on the U.S. Economy of Changes in Wait Times at Ports of Entry"[1] in March 2013. Their analysis of 17 major passenger land crossing POEs, 12 major freight crossing POEs, and four major passenger airport POEs, found that an increase or

---

[1] "The Impact on the U.S. Economy of Changes in Wait Times at Ports of Entry," National Center for Risk and Economic Analysis of Terrorism Events (CREATE), University of Southern California, released April 4, 2013 (dated March 31, 2013).

decrease in staffing at the POEs has an impact on wait times and, therefore, on the U.S. economy. More specifically, adding a single CBP Officer at each of the 33 studied border crossings equates to annual benefits of a $2 million increase in Gross Domestic Product, $640,000 saved in opportunity costs, and 33 jobs added to the economy per officer added.

More than half of the Nation's 329 official POEs are located along the U.S. land borders with Mexico and Canada. Most of the inspection facilities at our 167 LPOEs[2] were not designed to meet the post-9/11 security and operational missions of CBP. Rather, they were built to support the distinct operations of pre-DHS components, such as the U.S. Customs Service, the Animal and Plant Health Inspection Service of the U.S. Department of Agriculture, and the United States Immigration and Naturalization Service.

Today, CBP's operations entail sophisticated targeting and communication systems, state-of-the-art detection technology, and a cadre of professional law enforcement personnel to identify, screen, and inspect high-risk persons and cargo and maintain an efficient stream of cross-border travel and trade. However, the success of our operational strategy depends heavily on the condition and operational utility of the inspection facilities and the availability of CBP personnel.

Several LPOEs were built more than 70 years ago and require renovation or replacement to meet present-day operational and security standards. Many constructed as recently as 15 to 20 years ago also require significant modernization to address growing demands for additional processing capacity, new security requirements and enforcement technologies, and the need to maximize the efficiency of existing personnel and resources.

To construct and sustain CBP's LPOE inspection facilities, CBP works in close partnership with the GSA Public Buildings Service, which manages many of the LPOE facilities.

LPOE MODERNIZATION PLANNING PROCESS

CBP employs a multi-step process to plan for all LPOE modernization investments, whether planned for a CBP-owned or a GSA facility. This process includes gathering data using the Strategic Resource Assessment (SRA) process, evaluating identified needs at each POE location, conducting a sensitivity analysis on the initial ranking of needs, and assessing project feasibility and risk. The culmination of this process is a final prioritization of proposed modernization projects and the development of a capital investment plan in coordination with GSA. This capital investment plan divides the project list into feasible annual work plans that reflect the analytical conclusions and incorporate project phasing and funding requirements. CBP and GSA update the capital investment plan annually, taking into account any changes in DHS's mission and strategy, changing conditions at the LPOEs, and any other factors discovered in the course of projects already under way.

CBP and GSA work in close partnership with key Federal, State, and local stakeholders to construct and sustain CBP's LPOE inspection facilities. As a matter of coordination, CBP consults affected stakeholder agencies at the onset of project planning and continues this relationship throughout project development and execution.

As the facility operator at all LPOEs, including those owned or leased by GSA, CBP works in close coordination with GSA to identify long-term future investments for funding through the GSA Federal Buildings Fund (FBF). Through this collaborative project team approach, both agencies work to ensure that the available Federal funding is directed to the areas of greatest need within the GSA portfolio in accordance with the capital investment plan.

Although stimulus funding appropriated under the *American Recovery and Reinvestment Act (ARRA)*, Pub. L. 111–5, enabled CBP and GSA to fund many large-scale LPOE capital construction and facility improvement projects, significant additional investment is necessary to modernize the entire LPOE portfolio.

Infrastructure enhancements are critical to the improvement of trade and travel facilitation; these changes are necessary to support current traffic volumes and modern technology. Due to the budget environment over the past 4 years, there have been very limited investments towards modernizing POEs. However, thanks to the support of Congress, CBP received authority to accept reimbursement for activities and donations.

---

[2] LPOEs include all at-grade and bridge land port inspection facilities. These land port inspection facilities fall within the POE definition under 8 CFR § 100.4(a).

PARTNERSHIPS WITH THE PRIVATE SECTOR AND GOVERNMENT ENTITIES

CBP is frequently asked by our stakeholders to provide new or additional services at POEs across the country. We recognize the potential economic impact for new or expanded service, and we very much want to support these endeavors. However, due to budget restraints and limited resources, we are not always able to accommodate these requests.

A key aspect of CBP's three-pronged Resource Optimization Strategy is the exploration of partnering with the private sector through such activities as reimbursement and potential acceptance of donations. As part of CBP's Strategy, CBP received authority to enter into agreements under Section 560 of Division D of the *Consolidated and Further Continuing Appropriations Act, 2013,* Pub. L. 113–6 (Section 560); and Section 559 of Division F of the *Consolidated Appropriations Act, 2014,* Pub. L. 113–76 (Section 559).

Under Section 560, CBP received authority allowing the commissioner of CBP to enter into no more than five agreements under certain conditions to provide new or enhanced services on a reimbursable basis in any of CBP's non-foreign operational environments. CBP implemented this authority, entering into agreement with the participating locations[3] before the late December 2013 statutory deadline. In the first 6 months of the program, CBP was able to provide an additional 7,000 CBP Officer assignments and opened primary lanes and booths for an additional 18,000 hours at the request of our partners, increasing border processing throughput at U.S. air and land POEs under this program. In January 2014, CBP received additional authority under Section 559, which authorizes CBP to enter into partnerships with private sector and Government entities at ports of entry to reimburse the costs of certain CBP services and to accept donations of real and personal property (including monetary donations) and non-personal services.

Both provisions respond to CBP's efforts to find innovative approaches to meet the growing demand for new and expanded facilities and, in particular, the on-going modernization needs of CBP's LPOE portfolio.

Reimbursable Services Agreements

Section 559(e) expands CBP's authority, under a 5-year pilot program, to enter into reimbursable agreements similar to the fiscal year 2013 "Section 560" authority. This new authority allows CBP to support requests for expanded services including customs, agricultural processing, border security services, and immigration inspection-related services at POEs; salaries for additional staff; and CBP's payment of overtime expenses at airports. While there is no limit on the number of agreements CBP can enter into at CBP-serviced seaports or land border ports, only five agreements per year are currently allowed at new or existing CBP-serviced airports for each of the 5 years the pilot program is authorized. Additionally, the law stipulates that agreements may not unduly and permanently impact existing services funded by other sources.

CBP evaluates each Reimbursable Services Agreement (RSA) proposal based on a single set of objective and carefully-vetted criteria to ensure that final recommendations will be most beneficial to CBP, to the requesting parties, and to the surrounding communities. The main factors of consideration include the impact on CBP operations; funding reliability; community and industry concerns; health and safety issues; local/regional economic benefits; and feasibility of program use.

RSAs enable stakeholders to identify enhanced services needed to facilitate growing volumes of trade and travel at specific POEs, and enables CBP to receive reimbursement so that we can fulfill those requirements. The authority provides stakeholders and CBP the flexibility to meet situational or future demand for extended or enhanced services to secure and facilitate the flow of trade or travel at participating ports. At LPOEs this authority enables CBP to open and staff additional lanes or provide services for extended hours to reduce wait times and expedite commercial and personal traffic. At airports, RSAs enable CBP to staff additional booths and accommodate additional flights, or flight arrivals outside of standard operational hours, on an overtime basis. Accommodating additional flights means increased travel and tourism revenue for an airport or a region.

Donation Acceptance Authority

Section 559(f), the Donation Acceptance Authority, authorizes CBP and GSA to accept donations of real or personal property (including monetary donations) or non-personal services from private-sector or Government entities. Any donation accepted

---

[3] The Section 560 participating partners are the Dallas/Fort Worth International Airport Board, the City of El Paso, Miami-Dade County, the City of Houston/Houston Airport System, and the South Texas Assets Consortium.

may be used only for necessary activities related to the construction, alteration, operation, or maintenance of a new or existing POE, including but not limited to: Land acquisition, design, equipment, and technology.

The Donation Acceptance Authority legislation requires that CBP and GSA: (1) Establish criteria that identify and document their respective roles and responsibilities; (2) identify, allocate, and manage potential risk; (3) define clear, measurable objectives; and (4) publish criteria for evaluating partnership projects.

CBP has been coordinating closely with GSA to meet the Congressional deadline for making donation proposal evaluation criteria available to the public.

Both the Reimbursable Services Authority and the Donation Acceptance Authority enable CBP to build effective partnerships with stakeholders to address the port requirements necessary to support growing volumes of travel and trade.

CONCLUSION

The effective security of our Nation and facilitation of international trade and travel rely heavily on the health and operational utility of our inspection facilities. The CBP LPOE modernization strategy, in conjunction with GSA program and project management resources, ensures a reliable method for identifying future infrastructure needs and prioritizing projects at LPOEs. Innovative funding sources, such as the Reimbursable Services Authority and the Donation Acceptance Authority, are critical components of CBP's Resource Optimization Strategy. CBP views these authorities as an opportunity to proactively work with stakeholders and communities to identify business solutions for a variety of border management needs, and generate mutual benefits of the secure and efficient flow of travel and commerce.

The combination of highly-trained personnel, technology, and modernized facilities form the essential foundation for CBP's operational strategy, which every POE, large or small, must be able to support. CBP continues to evaluate and optimize its primary business processes and will further develop transformation initiatives to accomplish its mission more effectively and efficiently, through practices such as employing technology to streamline processes, expanding Trusted Traveler/Trader Program enrollment, increasing risk segmentation through enhanced targeting/pre-departure initiatives, and leveraging operational best practices.

Legitimate travel and trade play a critical role in the Nation's economic growth, and CBP recognizes its role in sustaining such growth. The number of international visitors and overall cross-border traffic is increasing, and CBP is aggressively working on modernizing our infrastructure and transforming the way we do business to more effectively and efficiently secure our Nation and improve our economy.

Chairwoman Miller, Ranking Member Jackson Lee, and Members of the subcommittee, thank you for the opportunity to testify today. I am happy to answer any questions you may have.

Mrs. MILLER. Thank you very much, Mr. Wagner.

Before we proceed with our witnesses' testimony, the Chairwoman would recognize Mr. Marino to ask his questions for the record, since apparently he has to leave. We appreciate his participation this morning.

Mr. MARINO. Thank you very much, Chairwoman.

Gentleman, I don't expect an answer from you right now, but if each of you would send me a—send the committee a written statement, you will be given the specific verbiage that I am going to read, so you don't have to worry about writing it down, okay? I thank you for being here.

Mr. Gelber, it is good to see you again.

It is a three-point question, so I will just read it for the record and then I will be on my way. To each of you, what is the purpose—excuse me—what is the process and how long does it take for GSA to begin work on a new port of entry, compared to the time frame to enhance, expand, or improve an existing established border operation once funding has been authorized?

Question No. 2: When existing ports of entry have tangible needs and even phased renovation or enhancement under way, why wouldn't those be completed before initiating new ports of entry, especially within the same traffic corridor?

Question No. 3: Does GSA/CBP have any obligation to complete projects that have been authorized and initiated at existing ports of entry before contemplating new ports of entry?

Madam Chairwoman, I thank you very much.

Thank you, gentlemen. Please get me that in writing.

Mrs. MILLER. I thank the gentleman.

Chairwoman now recognizes Mr. Gelber for his testimony.

STATEMENT OF MICHAEL GELBER, DEPUTY COMMISSIONER, PUBLIC BUILDINGS SERVICE, U.S. GENERAL SERVICES AD- MINISTRATION

Mr. GELBER. Good morning, Madam Chairwoman, Ranking Member Jackson Lee, and Members of the committee. My name is Michael Gelber and I am the deputy commissioner of the GSA's Public Building Service.

GSA's mission is to deliver the best value in real estate, acquisition, and technology services to Government and the American people. As part of this mission, GSA works with a range of Federal inspection agencies along our land borders. CBP is our primary partner in addressing border infrastructure, and GSA maintains a close partnership with CBP to meet its essential mission needs.

I look forward to outlining the importance of land ports of entry, our partnership with CBP, how the Government jointly prioritizes and executes port projects, and the challenges facing these investments.

GSA works closely with CBP to design, construct, maintain, and operate land ports of entry along our Northern and Southern Borders. These ports are integral to the Nation's trade and security.

GSA owns 102 land ports of entry along the Northern and Southern Borders and leases an additional 22 ports. CBP owns and operates 40 primarily smaller ports, mostly in rural, remote areas.

Given the crucial importance of these ports, GSA, in collaboration with CBP, has prioritized investment to modernize and upgrade these facilities. To ensure these investments address CBP's most pressing needs, GSA relies on the priorities established in CBP's 5-year plan for portfolio upgrades. This list of priorities can be—include expansion and modernization of existing land ports along with new port construction.

As CBP outlined, its process includes gathering data through a strategic resource assessment, ranking identified needs at each port, conducting a sensitivity analysis on the initial listing of these needs, assessing project feasibility and risk, and establishing an executable capital investment plan. In the current 5-year land port of entry construction plan, CBP identified six construction projects at land ports of entry, totaling more than $830 million in facility construction along the Northern and Southern Borders.

During the past 15 years, GSA has invested more than $1.5 billion to deliver more than 20 new land ports along our borders. In the past 4 fiscal years, the administration has requested more than $740 million in support of modernization of land ports to address CBP's most pressing needs.

15

Of these identified needs, Congress has provided approximately $295 million of these requests, all of which came in fiscal year 2014. The lack of full funding stalled critical modernizations and delayed land port upgrades that would secure our borders and improve the efficient flow of commerce with our neighbors in Canada and Mexico.

Given the consistent cuts to the port program, GSA has seen intense interest in finding alternatives to Federal appropriations to deliver high-priority port projects. When assessing any option, GSA and CBP must take a comprehensive look at the full life-cycle cost of a port.

These costs include the land where construction takes place, the infrastructure that supports the mission, the funds to staff the facility, and the sophisticated technology and equipment the Federal Government uses to ensure the Nation's security. If an alternative resource exists for one or more of these items, GSA and CBP likely still must find funding to address the full range of costs.

GSA has had some success in using alterative delivery methods to support land port projects in the past. For instance, GSA has a long-standing authority to accept unconditional gifts of real and personal property. GSA has used this authority multiple times when State or local governments, and in a few cases private-sector entities, have elected to donate property to GSA in order to realize economic benefits that comes with a new or expanded land port of entry.

For instance, at the San Luis II port in Arizona, GSA received a donation of land and utilities in support of the site to help make progress on a modernization project. In Donna, Texas, the local municipality donated money for design, land for the site of the port, and 180,000 cubic yards of fill dirt for construction. In Columbus, New Mexico, a private landowner donated approximately 10 acres of land to GSA near the port site for construction and a bypass road for commercial trucks.

Additionally, Congress has supported these efforts by providing for additional donation authorities, such as Section 559 of the fiscal year 2014 Consolidated Appropriations Act. These authorities present valuable opportunities to support port development. However, these resources have generally been utilized to make modest improvements to existing ports or defray the cost of a major modernization, not to deliver a full-scale upgrade of the type the administration has requested consistently in the President's budget.

GSA looks forward to working with Congress to further explore these and other flexible authorities and to continue to highlight the importance of these investments.

Thank you for the opportunity to speak with you today about our on-going partnership with the Federal inspection agencies, particularly CBP, as we address the Nation's security and economic needs along our borders. I welcome any questions you may have.

[The prepared statement of Mr. Gelber follows:]

PREPARED STATEMENT OF MICHAEL GELBER

JULY 16, 2014

INTRODUCTION

Good morning Chairwoman Miller, Ranking Member Jackson Lee, and Members of the committee. My name is Michael Gelber, and I am the deputy commissioner of GSA's Public Buildings Service.

GSA's mission is to deliver the best value in real estate, acquisition, and technology services to Government and the American people. As part of this mission, GSA maintains a close partnership with the Department of Homeland Security U.S. Customs & Border Protection (CBP) to meet that agency's space needs along our Nation's borders. CBP is our primary partner of the Federal inspection agencies stationed along our land borders.

I look forward to outlining the importance of Land Ports of Entry, our partnership with CBP, how the Federal Government jointly prioritizes and executes port projects, and the challenges facing these investments.

THE CRITICALITY OF LAND PORTS

GSA works closely with CBP to design, construct, maintain, and operate land ports of entry along more than 1,900 miles of border between the southern United States and Mexico and more than 5,500 miles of border between the northern United States and Canada. These ports are integral to the Nation's trade and security.

On a daily basis, about $2 billion in goods, 350,000 vehicles, 135,000 pedestrians, and 30,000 trucks cross the border at one of these 167 ports. Since 1990, the combined value of freight shipments between the United States and Canada and the United States and Mexico has increased 170 percent, growing an average of 8 percent annually. Additionally, approximately 23 million U.S. citizens cross the land borders into Mexico and Canada a total of nearly 130 million times each year. These statistics highlight the vital role of safe, secure, and modern land ports along our borders.

GSA owns 102 land ports of entry along the Northern and Southern Borders, leases or partially owns an additional 22. GSA's land port of entry inventory amounts to more than 5.5 million square feet of space. Additionally, CBP owns and operates 40 primarily smaller locations, mostly in remote, rural areas. The U.S. Department of Agriculture and U.S. Forest Service mutually own one land port of entry, and the National Park Service owns two ports.

GSA'S ON-GOING PARTNERSHIP WITH CBP IN SUPPORT OF LAND PORT MODERNIZATION

Given the crucial importance of these ports, GSA, in collaboration with CBP, has prioritized investment to modernize and upgrade these ports.

To ensure these investments address CBP's highest-priority needs, GSA relies on the priorities established in CBP's 5-year plan for portfolio upgrades. CBP employs a multi-step process to develop its 5-year plan. This list of priorities can include expansion and modernization of existing land ports along with new port construction.

As CBP has outlined, its process includes gathering data through Strategic Resource Assessment, scoring identified needs at each port, conducting a sensitivity analysis on the initial ranking of needs, assessing project feasibility and risk, and establishing an executable capital investment plan.

In the current 5-Year LPOE Construction Plan, CBP has identified six construction projects at land ports of entry totaling more than $830 million in facility construction along the Northern and Southern Borders.

During the past 15 years, GSA has invested more than $1.5 billion to deliver more than 20 new land ports along our Northern and Southern Borders. In the past 4 fiscal years, the administration has requested more than $740 million in support of modernization of land ports to address CBP's most pressing needs. Unfortunately, Congress has provided approximately $295 million of these requests, all of which came in fiscal year 2014. This has stalled critical modernizations and delayed land port upgrades that would secure our borders and improve the efficient flow of commerce with our partners in Canada and Mexico.

When a critical modernization project receives needed funding and, if required, the State Department issues a Presidential Permit, GSA and CBP work in close partnership with key Federal, State, and local stakeholders to construct and operate GSA-owned land port inspection facilities.

GSA and CBP consult with stakeholder agencies at the onset of project planning and continue this relationship throughout project development and execution. If a project involves a new border crossing and or a substantial modification of an existing crossing, GSA works closely with the State Department, which must determine whether the project is in the National interest justifying issuance of a Presidential Permit. GSA also works closely with the U.S. Department of Transportation's Federal Highway Administration (FHWA) and the transportation departments from the 15 Border States when planning border infrastructure projects. GSA and CBP are partners in the Border Master Planning process on the U.S.-Mexico border. In addition to coordination with State and local agencies, the border master planning process also includes Mexican (federal, state, and local) governments as well as other Federal agencies including State Department, DOT (FHWA, Federal Motor Carrier Safety Administration, etc.) and sometimes private partners as well (railroads for example). The connectivity of highways with the land ports of entry is critical to the safe and efficient flow of traffic and trade across our borders. In addition to working closely with domestic stakeholders, GSA also works closely with the Department of State to coordinate with Federal and local governments in Mexico and Canada.

ALTERNATIVE RESOURCES IN SUPPORT OF LAND PORT PROJECTS

Especially given the consistent cuts to the port program that I have previously mentioned, we have seen intense interest in finding alternatives to Federal appropriations to deliver high-priority port projects. Importantly, when assessing any options, GSA and CBP must look comprehensively at the full life-cycle cost of a port. This includes the land where construction takes place, the infrastructure that supports the mission, the funds to staff the facility, and the sophisticated technology and equipment CBP uses to ensure the Nation's security. If an alternative resource exists for one or more of these items, GSA and CBP likely still must find funding to address the full range of costs.

GSA has had some success in using alternative delivery methods to support land port projects in the past. For instance, GSA has long-standing authority to accept unconditional gifts of real and personal property from other public or private entities. GSA has used this authority multiple times when State or local governments, and in a few cases private-sector entities, have elected to donate land or other real property to GSA in order to realize the economic benefit that comes with a new or expanded land port of entry.

For instance, at the San Luis II port in Arizona, GSA received a donation of land and utilities in support of the site to help make progress on the modernization. In Donna, Texas, the city donated money for design, land for the site of the port, and 180,000 cubic yards of fill dirt for construction. In Columbus, New Mexico, a private landowner donated approximately 10.2 acres of land to GSA near the port site for construction and a bypass road for commercial trucks.

Additionally, Congress has sought to support these efforts by providing for additional donation and reimbursable service authorities. In fiscal year 2013, CBP received limited authority to enter into reimbursable service agreements with private-sector entities for the provision of certain inspectional services.[1] Congress expanded CBP's ability to execute these reimbursable service agreements in addition to broadening GSA's and CBP's donation acceptance authority in fiscal year 2014.[2]

These authorities present valuable opportunities to support port development. However, these resources have generally been utilized to make modest improvements to existing ports or defray the cost of a major modernization, not to deliver a full-scale upgrade of the type the administration has requested consistently in the President's budget.

We look forward to working with Congress to further explore these and other flexible authorities and to continue to highlight the importance of these investments.

CONCLUSION

Thank you for the opportunity to speak with you today about our on-going partnership with CBP and other Federal agencies to address the Nation's security and economic needs along our borders. I welcome the opportunity to discuss GSA's commitment to strategic investment in the Nation's land ports. I am happy to answer any questions you may have.

Mrs. MILLER. Thank the gentleman very much.
The Chairman now recognizes Mayor Leeser for his testimony.

---

[1] *Consolidated and Further Continuing Appropriations Act of 2013,* Pub. L. 113–6, Division D, Title V. Section 560.
[2] *Consolidated Appropriations Act of 2014,* Pub. L. 113–76, Division F, Title V. Section 559.

Again, sir, we certainly appreciate you traveling to Washington to testify before our committee today.

STATEMENT OF OSCAR LEESER, MAYOR, CITY OF EL PASO, TEXAS

Mayor LEESER. Oh, you have got to push the talk button, huh? Now you tell me.

Thank you, Chairwoman Miller, Ranking Member Jackson Lee, and all the committee Members, and of course, our Congressman in El Paso, who I have the highest respect for. Thank you very much for inviting me to testify today.

You know, our ports of entry are so important to our community, but it is not only our community in El Paso, and that is the important thing that we are here to discuss. One in every 24 jobs in the United States basically depend on U.S.-Mexico trade for their employment.

I will give you an example in Michigan, Chairwoman Miller. Your State alone represents 175,000 jobs, and it is the third-largest exporter of goods to Mexico, based on the 2012 information that I was able to receive, which is really important.

If we look at all the States that are represented here, which is Texas, California, South Carolina, Mississippi, Pennsylvania, we employ more than 1.5 million people and close to $120 billion in exports to Mexico. The lack of investment not only in the infrastructure but the manpower will create—will impact not only businesses, but also our ability, and that is so important.

When we talk about the investment in not only infrastructure but also the investment in the workforce, without the ability to invest in our ports, we would have—we would have delay in times, and that is what we are here to talk about. We are talking about the P3 program, the 560, which was the program that allowed El Paso to invest in itself, and that was one of the important things that we are talking about.

The way we were able to invest in ourselves was we were able to fund CBP Officers. Once we were picked as one of the five cities in the country to be able to go to this pilot program, we then met with the CBP Officers and we kind of looked at and said, "Where do we need to basically move forward? Where do we need to invest?"

We basically looked at the peak times and what peak times would make it more acceptable for us. So we basically now we meet on a timely basis; we meet every week and we talk about how we are improving times.

I will give you some examples. In pedestrians we have been able to decrease the wait time—I mean, we have been able to increase the people coming across our bridge by 18 percent, in vehicles by 30 percent, and commercial by 3 percent. But when you talk about we have increased those, we have also decreased wait time, you know, in those lanes.

So when we are able to fund these lanes and we were able to expedite the times where we are basically most needed, you could see that our investment in our community and the investment in the bridges increased because now people felt more comfortable. People felt comfortable being able to come across and not have to wait for

2 hours, or an hour, an hour-and-a-half, to be able to come across and be able to transport their goods.

We all know and we all understand that, you know, time is money in business, and if you are sitting on a bridge then you are going to find an alternate solution to a problem, which is we can't do business together because the wait time is too long. We can't sit there and wait for a couple hours.

So it has become very important for us to be able to identify, and identify the times we need. So our community invested in itself, and again, our pilot program just started on January 26, and El Paso along—between El Paso, Juárez, and Las Cruces we have 2.5 million people. It is a big region.

El Paso ranks among the top 30 largest exporters in the world. U.S. trade is more than $507 billion in 2013. When we are talking about 30 percent increase in vehicle traffic, one bridge alone had 54,000 more vehicles on that bridge, and the trade just in El Paso alone was over—almost $100 billion a year.

Again, I am not just talking about El Paso; I am talking about the whole country. It is so important when we talk about—again, we talk about Michigan. Michigan, 175,000 jobs rely on just El— you know, crossing into our borders.

Again, I thank you very much for the opportunity to speak. Your commitment not only helps El Paso, but the whole country.

[The prepared statement of Mayor Leeser follows:]

PREPARED STATEMENT OF OSCAR LEESER

JULY 16, 2014

Honorable Chairwoman Miller and Ranking Member Jackson Lee, allow me to start by thanking you for the opportunity to appear before you this morning. I would also like to thank my hometown Congressman, Representative Beto O'Rourke, for inviting me to be here and for his steadfast dedication to the constituents of the 16th District of Texas.

I appreciate the committee's interest in our Nation's international ports of entry and for your commitment to examine how the Federal Government can prioritize infrastructure investments. I am here today to help shed light on the need for investments at our international ports of entry for the economic security of not only El Paso, but the Nation as a whole.

One in every 24 workers in the United States depends on U.S.-Mexico trade for their employment. Chairwoman Miller, more than 175,000 jobs in Michigan alone rely on trade with Mexico, and your State was the third-largest exporter of goods to Mexico in 2012.

Taking a quick look at the other States represented here today, Texas, California, South Carolina, Mississippi, and Pennsylvania employ more than 1.5 million people whose jobs rely on trade with Mexico and close to $120 billion in exports to Mexico.

Lack of investment both in infrastructure and manpower at our ports of entry in El Paso can and will significantly impact business and trade in your State. A lack of investment at our international ports of entry is a lack of investment in your workforce.

One investment that has shown positive results in my community is one that your committee recently examined. Your committee looked outside of the box at how investments could be made at the ports of entry by allowing local communities to apply local funds to assist our Federal partners. Unfortunately, for years, there has been a lack of investment at our ports of entry, and local communities want to help by investing in themselves.

Through Section 560 of the 2013 Consolidated Appropriations bill, a pilot program was launched to allow communities like El Paso to help pay for additional overtime for Customs and Border Protection Officers at our international bridges. The city of El Paso was one of five pilot projects chosen for a 5-year test.

Once the city of El Paso was chosen to partner with CBP, city officials worked closely with our community partners to ensure their buy-in. I personally met with the maquiladora industry to ensure their satisfaction with the project. They understood the return on investment that they would see as a result of decreased wait times at our bridges. Furthermore, a 5-year pilot project reassured them there was enough time to work through any potential issues with new implementation of the program.

Outreach was also conducted to the overall community to ensure those who cross via foot or vehicle knew of the city's investment in helping open additional lanes during peak hours of operations at our bridges. Maquiladora employees, local university students, and shoppers, just to name a few, cross back and forth regularly, and it is important that we make their trips quick and easy.

El Paso City Council formally approved the partnership between the city of El Paso and CBP as well as approved a $0.50 increase to tolls at our bridges to create a dedicated funding source for the pilot. The city of El Paso's economic security depends on the flow of goods and people across our international ports of entry so it is important not only to ensure trade continues to flow freely but that people and vehicles can move quickly across the border.

The pilot started on January 26 of this year, and since the launch, we have seen very positive results. The city of El Paso has already invested more than $400,000 for close to 3,500 hours of overtime for the officers. Traffic volumes have increased substantially over the same period last year with an average increase for pedestrians at more than 18 percent, close to 30 percent for vehicles, and more than 3 percent with cargo. Even with volume increases across the board, we are seeing a decrease in wait times. We believe that as the program continues, we will see larger decreases in the bridge times.

Aside from the investment for additional officers at the bridges, in El Paso, there is a need for additional investment in the actual infrastructure. The El Paso-Juárez region is one of the largest bi-cultural border communities in the world that includes more than 2.5 million people. El Paso is ranked among the top 30 largest exporters in the world. With U.S.-Mexico trade totaling more than $507 billion in 2013, El Paso is a major player in this market with close to $100 billion of that trade crossing our international ports of entry.

A 30 percent increase in vehicular traffic means that CBP processed 54,000 more vehicles at one bridge for the same 1 month period over the prior year. Add to this the $100 billion of that trade annually crosses the El Paso international ports of entry and the strain on our bridges is immense.

In addition, our infrastructure is landlocked and we do not have the ability to add additional lanes to help with additional traffic. We can work together to ensure the lanes are fully staffed at peak times, but there are also a number of infrastructure improvement projects that have been identified to assist. My community, however, is again ready and willing to step to the plate to resolve these issues.

The Section 559 authorization would allow the city of El Paso to make the necessary upgrades to the infrastructure while allowing CBP and GSA to accept the improvements as a donation. The city of El Paso recently submitted a letter of intent to participate in this program, but I do not believe we should have to reapply. CBP should honor the current agreements with communities who have already showed their commitment to be a partner and allow the opportunity to work under the additional authority as well.

Aside from the Public-Private Partnership agreement in place, it should be noted that the El Paso community continues to show their commitment and desire to invest. Recently, City Council approved the inclusion of several projects in the overall capital investment plan for the city. The city is willing to invest the match dollars to execute large-scale projects to decrease wait times and increase trade across the United States. Congress must help our partnering Federal agencies by providing the funding for programs such as the Coordinated Border Infrastructure Program.

It is my belief that communities will help make the investment in areas such as this because of the impact lack of resources can ultimately have on a community. I urge you to continue thinking outside of the box for a way to help expedite trade across our country while at the same time investing in additional officers and infrastructure resources that will not only help the El Paso community but the greater U.S. population.

Thank you again for the opportunity to be with you this morning.

Mrs. MILLER. Thank you, Mr. Mayor.

I thank all the witnesses.

I will recognize myself for my questions here.

Actually, as I mentioned at the outset, the whole impetus of this hearing was to try to get the list—the elusive list that has not been forthcoming from CBP to this committee, despite numerous, numerous requests. As I say, we want to know who is on the list, how you construct the list, how you prioritize the various projects that are on the list. Obviously it is for Congress to determine appropriations to do all of these.

As we have mentioned, there are so many that need them but, like anything, you have to do a—I think Mr. Wagner called it a strategic assessment. Obviously you need to do a strategic assessment, but what is the criteria for making that kind of call for the construct of any of these infrastructure improvements that are necessary at our land ports of entry?

The mayor pointed out excellent points. We are talking about the jobs that are generated because of the commerce that is trading, and you mentioned about Mexico, and I am up on the Northern Border.

As I mentioned at the outset, Canada is actually our largest trading partner not only in my State, but in the Nation; Mexico, our second-largest trading partners. So it is critical that these ports of entry and the infrastructure be funded and appropriated and we move forward in a strategic fashion.

So I just got this list literally when you walked into the committee room today, so I am trying to on the fly here digest this list and understand exactly what to—how it was constructed. As I understand, this is a 4-year-old list.

So I guess my first question is: Is there an updated list? That would be my first question. Is there a current list? How can you be operating at 4 years later?

One thing in—that would certainly fly out at me is since in that time our President and prime minister of Canada have entered into the Beyond the Border agreement, which specifically talked about infrastructure improvements, including the Blue Water Bridge in my district, as a priority for the Nation—for both nations.

I guess that is my first question: Is there an updated list? Is there a current list or are you operating under a 4-year-old list?

Mr. SCHEID. So there are actually a couple of different lists. There is the larger list that was provided that is, as you would note, 4 years old. That was actually provided to Congress back in 2010. I apologize for any confusion about us not sending it back up again to you in advance of this hearing, but when I came across it this morning I brought up the entire assessments.

It was about 450 pages that explained all the ports and their needs; it explains the process by which we used to create that list. Given the work that goes into that, it is basically like a 5-year plan, although I don't think it is technically labeled as such.

What that does is it is, I mean, essentially a catalogue of the existing facilities, and it prioritizes based on about 60 different weighting factors where we have needs. Actually, I mean, it really takes the entire portfolio and identifies where there might be wait time issues, where there might be electrical code issues. I mean, it is kind of the gambit.

It takes into, as one of the members mentioned in the question, it takes into consideration where there has been planning investment already made by GSA or, you know, through Congress. So, for example, some of the projects that are on that list which are in our more recent list, which I will explain, are things like the Columbus, New Mexico port of entry, Alexandria Bay, where planning dollars have already been appropriated and we are looking for the construction dollars to complete those projects.

So that is the guiding kind-of 5-year plan.

In addition, the appropriators ask for and we provide what was referred to in Mr. Gelber's testimony as an executable 5-year plan. So as Ms. Jackson Lee pointed out, the report that came up in 2010 identified $6 billion worth of investment need. Recognizing that $6 billion isn't likely to get appropriated in probably my lifetime, we culled down a list that is executable.

That executable list is about $800 million. The projects on that list are San Ysidro phase 2; Calexico West phase 1; Alexandria Bay phase 1; Alexandria Bay phase 2; Columbus, New Mexico; and Calexico West phase 2; $838 million of investment.

The first three of those—San Ysidro, Calexico, Alexandria Bay phases—are in the 2015 President's budget. Alexandria Bay phase 2, Columbus, Calexico——

Mrs. MILLER. Okay. If I could—not to interrupt, but——

Mr. SCHEID. Sure.

Mrs. MILLER [continuing]. In the limited time here, first of all, in regards to all the documentation for the 5-year strategic plan, as you called it, if it is 450 pages we would certainly appreciate all of that documentation so that we are really on the same track here——

Mr. SCHEID. Yes.

Mrs. MILLER [continuing]. Understanding exactly what your criteria is and how you are moving. I have this list that you just went through, three of the first three you mentioned that were in the President's proposed budget agreement after several years of not having any proposals for ports of entry.

But if I look at—I mean, I am sure you have the whole raft of criteria, and I am just going to go back to the Blue Water Bridge because I am most familiar with that, but for the number of commercial vehicles of all of the ports of entry in the country, the first one is the Ambassador Bridge in Detroit; the second is Laredo; the third is Port Huron, Michigan, the Blue Water Bridge.

That is No. 3 in the Nation, and yet these that are on this list are—well one of them is not even on my list that goes—and I don't mean to be pitting one against the other. They don't even appear on the list of traffic that is going across, if we are considering—if we are worried about jobs, which I think certainly all of us on this side are very, very worried about jobs. That is part of our job is to make sure we do everything we can to improve the economy in the United States.

So thinking about trade and vehicles going across and commerce transiting these different things, again, I don't—I am just trying to understand what your criteria is. To me it would be hard to think that that is not one of at least the top three criteria you would take into consideration as you look at these various ports of entry.

How do you consider jobs and the economy?

Mr. SCHEID. So the various criteria basically fall out into four categories: Mission and operations, which would take into account some of the existing impact, so impact on the economy, wait times;

23

that is 35 percent of the score. Another 15 percent of the weighting goes into personnel and projected workload growth, so trying to look out into the future about what might be coming at those ports; that is 15 percent.

So 50 percent of the criteria is along the lines of, I think, what you are describing.

In addition, there are security and life safety considerations. Ports that have anything from ground water issues, electrical issues, 25 percent. Another space and site deficiency is 25 percent.

So certainly the impact on the economy, the wait times——

Mrs. MILLER. Well I would just—again, not to interrupt, but in the interest of time—I would just point this out then, for the record: The Blue Water Bridge, as I say, is the second-busiest border crossing on the northern tier. It is No. 3 for all the commercial vehicles, et cetera, that are going across. We have already done demolition. There is almost 60 acres of vacant property sitting in the middle of a busy city that has been done over the last decade.

The Congress has spent millions of dollars to help with our Michigan Department of Transportation through earmarks, back in the day of earmarks, actually, to get this site shovel-ready. It is totally ready—designed, et cetera. Ready.

Yet, on this list 14 years ago it is No. 22 on your list. So I—really, I take issue with how you are—obviously, with your criteria and I would like to discuss that a bit more with you, as well.

One other thing I would like to question before—I am going to keep taking all the time here, but I will also throw this out: We are very interested—and I appreciate some of the discussion about creative financing, as well, and taking advantage of some of the other private partner—public-private partnerships. Actually, on the Transportation Infrastructure Committee we intend to put into our 5-year National transportation reauthorization some language about P3s, whether it be at—to be utilized at ports of entries or roads or bridges or railroads or what have you.

But currently, under the Budget Act, to do something like that in many cases you have to upfront all of the money, and that is the way the—because of the scoring of the CBO. Obviously that negates the possibility of all kinds of P3s all over the country, and I guess I am just looking for some sort of response to that.

What is the best way for the Congress to go about trying to accommodate, in a changing world and a restricted environment, P3s? Would it require promulgating a new rule through GSA? Would it require a legislative change?

Mr. Gelber, perhaps you could discuss that or, if you don't know the answer immediately, it is certainly something we want to work with you on, because the Congress is very interested in doing these P3s.

Mr. GELBER. Sure. As you referenced, scoring rules or the Federal accounting rules that govern many of our projects do create some challenges for GSA. That would be something we would be happy to discuss with Congress about how to modify those. It is not simply a GSA matter, though; it is a larger Executive branch and a Legislative branch discussion.

Mrs. MILLER. Okay. Very well.

At this time the Chairwoman now recognizes the gentleman from El Paso, Mr. O'Rourke.

Mr. O'ROURKE. Thank you. Thank you, Madam Chairwoman, and thank you for bringing us all together on this very, very important issue. As you pointed out, we have issues in the districts that we represent that affect the economy, and issues of trade and mobility throughout the country. So I appreciate your leadership on this.

I would like to thank, even though she is not here, the Ranking Member for ensuring that we get our mayor, Oscar Leeser, here to share his experience and expertise on these issues of cross-border trade and mobility for legitimate trade and travel across our borders, and for his testimony and linking something that is important to us in El Paso—one out of every four jobs in the El Paso economy is connected to trade and travel across our bridge that link the United States and Mexico, but as he pointed out, that is connected to 6 million jobs in the interior of the United States—in Florida, and Pennsylvania, and South Carolina, and Michigan, and every other State in the union.

So this is important for us, but it is really important for this country to get it right.

So my first question for you, Mayor Leeser, is we are focused on capital projects and trying to understand how they are prioritized, how funding is allocated, what the time line is to complete them.

We have some wonderful ports of entry in El Paso, but our challenge, Madam Chairwoman, has been staffing these ports of entry. You can have the greatest capital projects plan and implementation in the world, but if you can't staff them you have really got a problem.

Thanks to the mayor and the city council with which he serves, El Paso was selected as one of five ports, competing against all land, air, and sea ports in this country, to pilot a program that allows our community, with scarce resources, to supplement what the Federal Government is obligated to do and increase and expand the staffing at those ports.

So, Mayor, I would like to give you a minute or 2 to discuss the need to complement what we are talking about here with capital projects with actually ensuring that these are staffed once they are finished. Talk about how important that is.

Mayor LEESER. Well, thank you very much for the question.

It is really important for us. So far, the program we—like I said earlier, it started January 26. Since January 26 the city of El Paso has invested a little over $400,000 and about 3,500 additional hours, which we fund to the CBP.

Like we talked about, it is very important to the city of El Paso for the success of this program, but the beauty of it is, you know, when you look at it, it is one of five pilot programs and it is very important for the success—for CBP for it to be successful for us so they can roll it out and hopefully move forward and make it a Nation-wide program.

So based on that, we have been able to really work hard together. Like I said, we meet weekly and we talk about, you know, where we are going to gauge the wait time and how we are going to staff the bridges properly and where, you know, which officers we will be able to fund. We are funding—basically what we are

funding is overtime right now, and like I said, we have spent a little bit—in 4, in 5 months we have spent a little bit over $400,000,
3,500 hours, and it is during the peak times in the afternoons right
now is what we are basically focusing on.

When we talked about a little bit—when we talked about the 18
percent increase in pedestrian traffic, 30 percent increase in vehicle
traffic, and 3 percent increase in commercial traffic, that increase,
in my opinion, is based on funding of these officers and being able
to open these lanes and make it easier to do business in the United
States—not only El Paso. I think that is the important part that
we need to understand today: We are not talking about El Paso;
we are talking about the United States and where it just comes in.

Being able to have that type of increase and still decrease wait
time is incredible, and we will continue every week to meet and
kind-of gauge where that peak times are and where we need to
continue to fund those officers.

Mr. O'ROURKE. Thank you, Mayor.

For Commissioner Wagner, in fiscal year 2015 I believe El Paso
and Buffalo have been selected for another pilot program, which
would give CBP ownership-like control of ports in those districts.
Can you talk a little bit about how that is going to affect these
bridges, the processes and procedures on them, and what it will do
to address the issue that the mayor raised, which is that if we can,
in a lawful, secure manner, expedite legitimate trade and travel,
that increases jobs throughout this country.

So what will this pilot program offer for us, given those considerations?

Mr. WAGNER. Thank you. That pilot project entails the delegation
of authority for the maintenance of the facilities, and I will defer
to the gentleman on my left for the more specifics of it, but it allows CBP, then, to do the routine maintenance up to a specific
threshold of funding levels, and then we will have direct control
and direct access of maintaining the facility itself.

But as far as just facilitating and growing the trade and travel,
which we agree 100 percent with you, is so vital to our Nation, it
is the expansion of the public-private partnerships and the technology and, you know, the processes that we impose and making
sure they are as efficient and secure as possible. Just to echo some
of the mayor's sentiments about the great productive relationship
we have had with the five locations participating in the reimbursable services and the transparency that we are trying to show in
delivering the right data, the right information, the right metrics
and measurements in coordination and agreement with the entities
requesting these services, so everyone understands exactly what
they are paying for and what were the benefits that were seen out
of that.

We are off to a great start with all the locations in doing this.
So, like the mayor mentioned, we are hopeful to continue the expansion of this.

But I will defer to Mr. Schied for a second.

Mr. SCHEID. Briefly, the pilot delegation that we have been nego-
tiating with GSA would—what we are looking for is the ability to
make adjustments—minor—to the operations of the port as needed
when situations arise, so it is to accommodate the mission of the

port more readily as well as the basic operations upkeep, maintenance of the facility.

Mr. O'ROURKE. Thank you.

As I yield back, I would just ask that you give us an opportunity to meet with you to see what we can do, given this change, to capitalize on some of the opportunities to enhance the flow of legitimate trade and travel. So thank you.

Madam Chairwoman, I yield back.

Mrs. MILLER. Thank the gentleman.

The Chairwoman now recognizes the gentleman from Pennsylvania, Mr. Barletta.

Mr. BARLETTA. Thank you.

Thank you all for participating today.

Just this morning in the Transportation and Infrastructure Committee we approved 27 GSA resolutions authorizing projects in GSA's capital improvement program for fiscal years 2014 and 2015. This includes three port of entry projects in New Mexico, New York, and California.

At Calexico, California over 11,000 privately-owned vehicles and nearly 13,000 pedestrians enter the United States every day. Today we approved updating this 1974 facility to accommodate modern inspection technology for private vehicles and improve the pedestrian crossing.

This is in addition to border projects we approved in February for Laredo, Texas and San Ysidro, California, which is the biggest land border crossing in the country. So I know the Transportation and Infrastructure Committee and the Homeland Security Committee stand ready to work with you to get these critical projects not only approved but also moving forward.

I am going to follow up on a question Chairwoman Miller brought up, Mr. Gelber. I recognize that the fiscal year 2014 Consolidated Appropriations Act gave CBP new authority to use public-private partnerships, frequently called P3s, for ports of entry.

Now, our ports of entry are centers of major economic growth, as goods are transported back and forth across the border. Last year I visited San Ysidro and saw traffic jams created by insufficient infrastructure. Excessive lines of commercial vehicles at the ports of entry are wasted economic opportunities.

The communities and industries around these ports of entry are ready to invest in the much-needed infrastructure.

I sit on a special P3 panel with Chairwoman Miller, and we have been working to better understand the role public-private partnerships can play in leveraging private capital as well as private sector efficiency and innovation. In a Transportation and Infrastructure Committee's special public-private partnership panel we have repeatedly run into a brick wall regarding the budgetary scoring of public-private partnerships.

The Transportation and Infrastructure Committee is not the only committee to face such scoring roadblocks for P3s. I have also heard that the scoring is a problem for some veterans and defense projects as well.

Could you discuss with how these budgetary scoring problems impact P3 infrastructures for border crossing projects? If you could explain how——

Mr. GELBER. The challenge regarding scoring or Federal accounting rules is that whenever the Federal Government is engaged in investment in a particular project, the costs of that investment are assembled, if you will, in the first year of that project. So if the Federal Government is going to be building a facility for $250 million, the entire cost of that project has to be accounted for in the initial year even if the expenditure occurs over multiple years. If the Federal Government is going to be leasing a project from a private entity, and let's say hypothetically that lease over the course of 20 years is $300 million, the entire cost of that $300 million lease has to be accounted for in the first year even though the rent payments occur on a monthly basis over the 10 or 20 years of that lease.

So the challenge that we have with the budgetary impact, the scoring rules that you reference, in effect take money away from our budget authority in order to implement many of these projects. I hope I have given some justice to these rules. It is a rather complex area in terms of how Federal accounting and Federal budgeting is tallied, if you will.

Mr. BARLETTA. Thank you.

Mr. Wagner, I know your agency is working to build new port of entry facilities. When I was at the border earlier this month a Border Patrol Agent expressed to me that the Border Patrol has a difficult time patrolling some areas between ports of entry due to a lack of roads and infrastructure.

How is your agency working to prioritize building roads and infrastructure between new and existing port of entry facilities to better help agents do their job? What can Congress do to help?

Mr. SCHEID. So that would fall into a class of assets that CBP owns, and absolutely the roads, I think, are some of the most vital tools that Border Patrol Agents get out of the overall infrastructure improvements, which includes lighting, fencing, but certainly access and maintaining roads is critical to their ability to do their job.

The prioritization of that largely comes from the Border Patrol. They are identifying a mission need—areas where they prioritize the greatest need for access. My office then works with them to deal with land issues, the funding issues that come with that. But there is a process we use to prioritize new investment and maintenance, as well, into infrastructure, roads, and fence.

Mr. BARLETTA. Mrs. Miller, could I just ask one quick question?

Mr. Wagner, as Customs and Border Protection modernizes and builds new port of entry facilities how does it plan to prioritize and implement a biometric entry-exit system, as required under the current law?

Mr. WAGNER. So we have recently opened our test facility in Landover, Maryland, in partnership with the DHS Office of Science and Technology. We will be spending the rest of this calendar year looking at different types of biometrics and different types of operational uses where we can implement them.

Principally going to be focused on the air environment right now for commercial air travelers, but with an eye towards how would this also work at the land border without creating gridlock and congestion even more so than there is now? Then, you know, looking at the additional challenges that the land border is having—

28

not really having any facilities that would support stopping cars, collecting a biometric, and figuring out exactly that concept of operations, how to do it.

So we have started this essential work in evaluating the different technologies that are out there and then working through some of the different concepts of operation on how we would implement that. But, like we have spoken before, I mean, we see it as critically important. We want to collect the information. We just want to make sure we are collecting it in a way that doesn't create gridlock and shut down travel and trade in a way that it jeopardizes our authority to even collect it.

But we do realize the importance of it, and we are going to figure out a way.

Mr. BARLETTA. I hope we do. You know, John F. Kennedy—I like to use the example, John F. Kennedy in the 1960s, before we even had a space program, promised that we would put a man on the moon and bring him back before the end of the decade. Lo and behold, the great United States of America was able to do that.

We have been trying to figure this out for 25 years and we haven't done so yet, so I hope we get lucky and try to get it done, because I believe it is critical to our National security that we are able to do this if we are going to have true border security.

Thank you.

Mrs. MILLER. Thank the gentleman.

The Chairwoman now recognizes the gentleman from South Carolina, Mr. Duncan.

Mr. DUNCAN. Thank you, Madam Chairwoman.

Mr. Wagner and Mr. Schied, I just want to say that the week of the 4th I was in Montana on a family vacation and took the initiative to set up a tour at the Port of Roosville—Highway 93, north of Kalispell, north of Eureka, border crossing with Canada—that I had been through on numerous times in the past. I had seen the infrastructure changes there from an old port of entry of two lanes and an old National Park Service-type booth that was there, if you have been to Glacier or other places, very similar historically, but now we have a 21st Century modernized facility there at the Port of Roosville.

The area port director for that region, Daniel Escobedo, APD Escobedo, did a great job—and the men and women that are serving up there are serving very well. So I give a shout out to them, and I appreciate them taking the time to visit.

I shared with them, Madam Chairwoman, that a lot of the focus in our country right now is on our Southern Border, but those on our Northern Border haven't been forgotten. I shared the fact that you, being in a Northern Border State, shared that interest, as well, and that we have talked about, "Don't forget about the Northern Border." So I shared that, that those folks have not been forgotten, and I asked APD Escobedo to share that with all the folks—267, I think, people under his charge.

But one thing I noticed while I was up there is they are focused on ag issues, what items could be brought across from Canada, to the point of inspecting picnic baskets from Canadians coming into Montana to maybe go to Glacier or one of the natural resources there in Montana.

They can't bring citrus into the country. They can stop at a grocery store and buy American citrus, but that is a concern of theirs. They are concerned about the aquatic invasive species, working with the Montana Fish and Wildlife Service who had representatives there in the facility to inspect boats, not bring aquatic—all that is important, and I applaud them for that.

But I think about our Southern Border about—we have no idea what is coming into this country at this point. We have a porous Southern Border and folks are coming across, human smuggling, not just the children but others that are exploiting this situation that we have when we have no idea what is coming into our country, but yet we have got brave men and women at our Northern Border and they are looking in picnic baskets.

The juxtaposition of those two things struck me as a wow moment, going, you know, we are looking at boats and making sure all the water is drained out of the live well and there is not a bit of aquatic grass or anything on a boat that is coming into Montana, or making sure there is not an apple in a picnic basket or a citrus fruit of any sort. But yet we don't know what is coming across our Southern Border.

One thing I was amazed at, talking about infrastructure, because I hadn't thought about this, Madam Chairwoman, and maybe you have, but the buses of tourists that come back and forth across the border. There was, in the Port of Roosville, an area for buses to pull in because it is cold up in Montana in the winter time, where every passenger has to get off that bus; every passenger has to have a verifiable passport; every bag has to be connected with a passenger, and if there is a bag that isn't connected it is quarantined and it is searched.

Just the monumental effort of doing that in inclement weather is quite a challenge, because our Border Patrol Agents—not just the guys out on the horses and on the ATVs and in the trucks patrolling the border, but the guys in the Border Protection services, you have got to get it right 100 percent of the time. The bad guys only have to get it right once to do great harm to this country. They only have to get it right once to bring a nefarious item into this country that could be used to do great harm.

You guys have to get it right 100 percent of the time in order to protect this country, and that is not lost on me. Drugs, human smuggling, contraband, and nefarious items are things I wrote down here that they have got to look out for.

I watched at that border the border agent, what questions he asked, how he verified the documents, inspection of the vehicle. I watched him do it over and over and over, and I am so thankful that those guys are dedicated to keeping me and my family safe, to keeping my country that I love so much safe.

But I think about all the porous areas in the south that are being exploited every day and I go: Why can't America get this? Let's build a fence. Let's secure our Southern Border. Let's do the simple things to secure this Nation.

Let's support the guys that are wearing the blue standing at those booths inspecting those cars for the apples and everything else. Let's support them. I think support means we secure our Southern Border, as well.

I kind of tie my comments to the gentleman from El Paso and to the mayor, because—but with caution—because I understand the trade issues. I understand the need for better infrastructure for legitimate trade.

But I have got to couple that with the threats to this Nation and the violation that we see on our Southern Border every day of our National sovereignty. Laws are on the books for a reason. You guys are doing your job at the border, at the ports of entry because there are laws that require you to do that to keep our country safe and to protect our citizens.

But other laws are being ignored and the Border Patrol is not being supported with regard to the exploitation of our Southern Border. So we have got to get this right as America.

We can talk about the humanitarian issue with the children coming across, and I am very sympathetic to that. I want to try to help the children.

But I also want to repatriate them back to their families and their homes and their countries of origin because they came here illegally. Regardless of their stature, regardless of their age, or regardless of why they came to our country, they still came illegally.

So I want to try to support you.

I want to try to support legitimate trade, Mr. Mayor. I agree that we have got to get that right, as well, because there are tremendous opportunities for American businesses and foreign businesses wanting to do business in this country.

There is a legitimate need, Madam Chairwoman, for us to know what the infrastructure needs are, for us to get actually a prioritization of what CBP and DHS wants as far as, you know, where they are going to spend this money, how they are going to spend this money, how they are prioritizing. Do they build an infrastructure at the Port of Roosville or Sweetgrass in Montana, or do they focus that in El Paso or Nogales or somewhere like that, where there is a lot of trade?

So that is why it is so important for you guys to come and bring the information that is necessary for our oversight function and for us to say, "Hey, when we go to an appropriations process this is why. Convince us that this is how you want to spend the money, this is where the need is in this country, and let us go to bat for you." But without that information in a timely manner it is difficult for Members of Congress that may be in agreement with you to actually do our job and to actually go to bat for you.

So in absence of that information, you are not going to have a whole lot of friends on this dais because we don't have the information needed to make necessary and correct decisions for this country.

You have a challenge. The Northern Border is huge. The Southern Border is huge.

I will leave this information with you: We spend approximately $3.2 million per mile to build a four-lane interstate highway in a rural area in this country, on average. Think about that for a minute. A four-lane interstate highway—purchasing right of way, grading, paving, fencing, signage—approximately $3.2 million.

We spend about $4 million to $6 million per mile to build a fence in this country—let me back up. I got that reversed. Four million

31

dollars to $6 million to build a highway, four-lane highway; $3.2 million to build an interstate—I mean, to build a fence. It is not that big a difference, is what I am getting at.

So if we spend $4 million to $6 million per mile to build a four-lane highway and $3.2 million per mile to build a fence, why not just build a four-lane highway? I am being a little bit tongue-in-cheek facetious there, but what I want to point out is there is a 700-mile border.

The Secure Fence Act 2006 said build a fence. If you built a fence at $3.2 million per mile for 700 miles that comes to $2.24 billion. Good golly, if you did the—if you really looked into how much this Government blows every day and every year, surely we can appropriate $2.24 billion to build a 700-mile fence.

With that I yield back.

Mrs. MILLER. Thank the gentleman.

The Chairwoman now recognizes the Ranking Member, Ms. Jackson Lee.

Ms. JACKSON LEE. Let me thank the Chairwoman. This committee is probably noted for its bipartisanship, but we are collegian in our disagreement.

Mayor, coming from your great State, as I do, I don't have the same perspective, and frankly, totally disagree with the assessment of my good friend.

We have not had a catastrophic terrorist act on our soil since 9/11. We have had incidences that have been a result of many issues. In particular, we are reminded of the huge tragedy in Boston, and that was, in fact, a failure of intelligence and communication that we know we have to continue to correct.

We have had incidences of the shoe bomber, and that was thwarted. As I have been privileged to be in Classified briefings, any number, because of the new Homeland Security Department, covering all of the gamuts, from Mr. Wagner's team to Border Patrol Agents to ICE Officer to TSO Officer and others, our intelligence units have contributed to the safety of your city.

Those of us who live on the border in Texas don't particularly have our hair on fire unless provoked by individuals who want to make an international issue. I am always reminded of the contiguous countries in Europe and elsewhere where there is a free flow of individuals and they don't necessarily count the border issue as the basis for terrorism.

As we have seen here, there is home-grown terrorism; there are issues going on in places like Syria and Iraq that generate jihad and people moving from places; there are Americans who have become radicalized on the internet; we have had tragic incidences in our States at Fort Hood.

So I think we have to be very careful to have a mayor from El Paso and begin to describe circumstances that are really not realistic.

Mayor, let me ask you a simple question: Do you want your city to be secure?

Mayor LEESER. Well absolutely, but one thing that I do want——

Ms. JACKSON LEE. If I may ask the questions——

Mayor LEESER. Yes, ma'am.

Ms. JACKSON LEE. Just yes or no, you want your city to be secure?

Mayor LEESER. Yes, ma'am.

Ms. JACKSON LEE. Do you believe that your city, which is a local jurisdiction, continues to have a very positive relationship with those who are responsible for the border? You have a city that has a port of entry. You have a number of—you have a team, you have a large conglomerate of Border Patrol Agents, and you have CBP. Do you feel there is a strong working relationship there?

Mayor LEESER. Yes, ma'am.

Ms. JACKSON LEE. Do you feel that this hearing that is about infrastructure, that improved infrastructure and technology and other contributions to that border structure would be helpful to your city?

Mayor LEESER. Yes, ma'am.

Ms. JACKSON LEE. Do you believe that you have a vibrant exchange of business, both in terms of Americans traveling to Mexico and beyond and those coming into the United States who are engaged not in terrorist and/or criminal activities but engaged in trade, is that a vigorous part of your city's culture and economy?

Mayor LEESER. Yes, ma'am.

Ms. JACKSON LEE. So this hearing speaks to the infrastructure of trying to improve that circumstance. Is that positive for you?

Mayor LEESER. Yes.

Ms. JACKSON LEE. So let me then yield to you, because you wanted to expand. My interpretation that our hair is not on fire, that we are used to the ingress and egress of individuals, both Americans and others, is that accurate? Were you going to comment on that? Is that accurate?

Mayor LEESER. Well, what I was going to comment on, that, you know, you talk about El Paso, which is population of a little over 800,000 people, and based on FBI reports, we are the safest city over 500,000 in the United States. That is very important to—based on all the questions you just asked me—to put out there, that we are the safest city in the country.

Ms. JACKSON LEE. I think that is an important point. I join the Chairwoman in the importance of this hearing, but I take great pains and great opposition to the characterization of our border—Southern Border—and the characterization of our State.

Mr. Wagner, let me ask two questions: No. 1, can you—do you need more resources, as we move into the appropriations process, to supplement some of your staffing needs? Specifically in terms of infrastructure, as well, what aspect of infrastructure would you welcome—technology, rebuild of ports of entry? What would you welcome?

Mr. WAGNER. Thank you. Actually, all of the above——

Ms. JACKSON LEE. Very good. We are going to fight for you.

Mr. WAGNER. Thank you. Thank you for your support on this. You know, we have submitted with the 2015 budget proposal a need for 2,373 additional CBP Officers. You know, we have a workload staffing model which has taken every action CBP Officers do at a port of entry and it has quantified that data, and it translated into work hours that are needed and into personnel that can actually accomplish that work. That was submitted as part of the administration's 2015 proposal.

Technology is a tremendous help with that, and we have deployed a lot of really creative technology packages, starting at the land border with the RFIED, the radio frequency identification enabled travel documents, that allow us to query—perform a name-based computer query of every single person, almost, crossing the border. You know, before that we were querying about 5 percent of the people crossing the border; we are now into about 97 percent, based on that technology.

You have seen at the airports, like in Houston, the global entry kiosks, the self-service kiosks. We work closely with the city and the airlines to put in these automated passport control kiosks to help travelers do part of the inspection process rather than just sitting and waiting in line.

So really we have had some really creative approaches to the technology support, but it can't replace what the officer then brings—the CBP Officer brings to that process to determine a person's purpose and intent of travel. That is something we haven't found a piece of technology that can determine that for us, you know, and you need the officer's judgment to question a person and determine, what is the purpose and the intent of what they plan to do in the United States, to ferret out those that do intend to do us harm.

Like you mentioned, the threat is still out there and——

Ms. JACKSON LEE. Absolutely.

Mr. WAGNER [continuing]. There are still those people out there, they are still plotting against us. You are right, you know, we have to remain vigilant to do that.

Now, the facilities themselves—better facilities will help us accomplish that work better and more efficiently. If we can move the compliant people out of the way and get them to their destinations and onward and be productive, that helps us focus in on who are the bad actors amongst the group, what are the dangerous things coming in.

So having facilities that help support those programs that allow us to remove the compliance populations away and then help us be able to better focus in on the areas in a risk assessment process on how to do that, so——

Ms. JACKSON LEE. Thank you.

Mr. WAGNER [continuing]. It is a combination of personnel, technology, and facilities that will help us do it. Thank you for your support.

Ms. JACKSON LEE. The Chairwoman has been gracious in our time.

I just want you to, if you would in writing, because I have a quick question for Mr. Gelber—welcome, sir—from GSA. In writing, give us how the 559 private partnership—private-public partnerships are working.

Then can you just answer this: In the course of your work dealing with the individuals coming across, is the Wilberforce bill dealing with human trafficking and dealing with unaccompanied children and their rights, has that interfered what you do in your work?

Mr. GELBER. It hasn't interfered; it is just the challenge of the logistics of taking the children, holding onto them until Health and Human Services can respond——

Ms. JACKSON LEE. So we need to give you help on that end——

Mr. GELBER. Yes.

Ms. JACKSON LEE [continuing.] For the expedited response to get those children away from you——

Mr. GELBER. It is—right.

Ms. JACKSON LEE. Pardon me? I am——

Mr. GELBER. It is the capacity of the system and the process to handle the influx of——

Ms. JACKSON LEE. I will just ask him to put it on the record.

Mr. Gelber, if you could write on the record—the Chairwoman has said she has a markup and I thank her for her time. If you could just give us in writing what your assessment is of GSA's continued operation of some of those areas—ports of entry.

Sorry for the fact that I can't get on the record, but I want to thank you for your service.

Mr. GELBER. Thank you very——

Ms. JACKSON LEE. We will be in touch directly.

Mrs. MILLER. Thank the gentlelady.

The Chairwoman now recognizes the gentleman from Florida, Mr. Clawson.

Mr. CLAWSON. I want to assure Ms. Jackson Lee that I like your State a lot. I like the border.

Mayor, thank you for coming. You have an incredible challenge on your hand, but you have a wonderful city and a wonderful area, and I know a little bit about it, and I am glad you came today.

Ports of entry are important to Florida in so many ways, so this is something that is important to my constituents. I understand a little bit about what you all are talking about with respect to trade and life on the border.

I have managed factories in the Nuevo Laredo, in Monterrey, in Chihuahua, Apodaca, Allende. I know a little bit about this area, and I have lived 100 miles south of the Laredo, Texas border myself.

It is not only a business and services question, of course, but it is also a humanitarian question, as so many people depend on that transporter traffic for their daily life, from education to what they buy to what they sell. So what you all are doing, I guess I am saying first of all, is so important to our country and to our well-being not only in terms of security, which we hear so much about, but also I am agreeing with you with respect to commerce.

I learned quite a bit today. I have probably been here less than you have—many of you. But I am—I feel a little bit in the dark. In my background I would say that I feel like I have come to a board meeting without a board book, and so I am hearing management tell me that they would like to make capital expenditures and move their strategic plan along, and I do not have data that shows me how they have earned it.

I am not doubting that you have earned it. Mayor and the rest of you, when you speak anecdotally about some of the improvements and how you are getting more throughput through the border, I am not doubting that at all.

But if you want my support for more money I need to know how you have earned the money in the past. That is called fiduciary or constituent responsibility.

So speaking for myself, it is hard to show up at a meeting with no data about previous projects, about future projects, and about what you have earned without capital expenditures, because all management is responsible for improvements that aren't capital expenditure-related. I am not making the point that I am saying that you are not doing that.

What I am saying is that I need some professional summary data here so I can make my own assessment of it beyond anecdotes that I am not—that I do not doubt, but I need more fulsome information to make a rational financial as well as humanitarian choice for these sorts of projects.

So if I had, in my words, a strategic plan that was put in front of me with what your projects are, what the criteria are, and how you have earned it from your improvements of the past, it would help me make a decision. Because without that I am not sure I have a meaningful opinion, other than to just listen to what you are saying and say it sounds good.

So if any of you would like to respond to that, that would be great. But without more data it is hard for me to say yea or nay or anything you are asking for because I feel like you have left me in the dark.

Mayor LEESER. I would like to respond to that, sir.

Mr. CLAWSON. Yes, sir.

Mayor LEESER. Congressman, one thing that the 560 program does, it gets the community of El Paso and the citizens of El Paso to invest in the P3, the private partnership. We have committed $1.5 million to help fund officers and pay overtime to be able to expedite.

One thing about the 560, we will not—our job is not to tell them how to do their job; our job is to help them fund their officers to help us bring trade and open up those lanes for the city of El Paso and the whole United States, really. Our investment by our community and our citizens is really an investment in the United States and an investment in the workforce not only in El Paso but Nation-wide.

So we have invested $1.5 million to add additional agents and add—and pay for additional hours. In just a few—almost 5 months we have—from the sense of El Paso paid a little over $400,000 and 3,500 hours have been funded.

One thing we do ask also is the 559 program, which was referred to, that we allow us, based on our investment and our commitment—because we are landlocked in El Paso; we can't add additional lanes; we can't add any additional capacity. So we can help fund the officers, but we also would like not to have to reapply for the 559 program but give us the ability to help fund some infrastructure, again, to make that—to be able to make it easier, again, on our community and our country.

Thank you.

Mr. CLAWSON. Right. I want to be supportive, but I need to know how your program fits into the overall strategic plan of the CBP. I think that would make sense for you guys, right?

Mr. SCHEID. Absolutely. I think that there is the data that is there, and we are certainly happy to provide that to you, both from the facility standpoint but also the workload staffing model that we use to justify the request for additional officers. I think there are also independent assessments that have been done that I think give you a lot of that sort of business case that you are looking for, and we would be certainly happy to follow up with that.

Mr. CLAWSON. I acknowledge much of the information may be there, and since I have only been here a few days I may not know where it is. I would always say the way to manage a board of directors is to make it easy for them and don't make it hard for them.

If you want to make it easy for me, bring me data that I can understand that shows you are doing your job, you are taking care of taxpayer dollars, you are defending taxpayer dollars, and when we give you a dollar you are making great productivity out of that dollar. Make that case. Show me how the mayor's program fits into that and you are much easier to have allies.

But if I am kind of lost in data up here, I am sorry. We are doing a lot of other things here and we have got to—you have got to help us out a little bit. If you do, I am all ears.

I yield.

Mrs. MILLER. Thank the gentleman very much. Again, we certainly welcome you to the committee.

Even though you have only been here a short period of time, you make a very excellent point about information. It is difficult—I don't care what your business is, but particularly if you are a Member of Congress trying to make determinations about spending the taxpayers' dollars and you are trying to do it in a vacuum without the information.

I will just point out again, we did not have this list that we are now looking at. For the last several months we have been asking for the list. So appreciate we did get it 10 minutes before the hearing started.

Before we close, I just have one follow-on question, as I have tried to digest this list—the 4-year-old list. I think I was told that how you weight this to prioritize, et cetera, about half of it is economics; and then the other half, I think, is sort of flow. I am looking at your priority here, so half economics, half flow, essentially. You have got all these other criteria there.

Yet, by that measure, looking at some of these that have been—these—two that were funded in the President's budget this year, and then a couple of others that are one the—your list that you provided us here today for capital priorities, one of them is not even on my list of commercial vehicle flows, and yet they are next up to get funded. I am just telling you again, here is the Blue Water Bridge in Port Huron is No. 3, and we are 22 on the list.

So when you talk about how you prioritize, what you testified today does not bear out. I cannot make the numbers at least gel in my mind here if you are looking at economics and traffic flow for how you have prioritized this list.

Again, I just go back to the Blue Water Bridge because, in addition to the actual flow and the economics, it has been identified by both President Obama and Prime Minister Harper, the leaders of the two nations that are impacted, as a priority in the Beyond the

Border agreement, unlike these others that don't appear on many of these other lists.

So I don't understand this. Can you help me out? It doesn't make sense, of what you have testified to how you have come up with this list.

Understanding that you do have to have long-term, 5-year strategizing here, do you plan to update this list? If you do, can you share that with us as well? Are you changing your criteria?

Mr. SCHEID. So yes, we will plan—do plan to update that list. It is now, as you point out, several years old. Many of the projects on that list have been worked. In some cases we continue to look for public-private partnerships, smaller improvements that, in the absence of—the several years where we had no capital investment appreciably coming in, trying to find smaller incremental improvements—stacked booths, those kinds of things—to do what we could to alleviate the wait times. But it is absolutely time to update that list.

I think in terms of the criteria, the—I think a lot of the criteria do stand: Economics being an important driver, safety—having the right——

Mrs. MILLER. Economics being half, right? I think you testified to that, approximately—a heavy weight.

Mr. SCHEID. A heavy weight.

Also, the overall mission need of that facility. So there is the enforcement aspect of the mission that has to be accommodated there. So the mission includes both the—facilitating the flow of traffic as well as being able to do the enforcement activities. I think those criteria are good.

I think in addition to it we—something that didn't really exist a couple of years ago is the public-private partnership. I think figuring out a way to take those opportunities into account and to, you know, bring that new 559 into this process, where communities have investment that they can bring to the table and how should that impact the scoring of—or the ranking of the list.

Because a community may want to bring resources to the table and perhaps donate the capital, the overall lifetime life cycle of that facility is going to be—well——

Mrs. MILLER. Okay. Again, I just—what you are testifying, as you use this criteria and the way that the construct of this list looks like to me is a complete disconnect, I believe, at least in my mind.

Let me just ask you one other question. Again, I am not trying to pit one area against another——

Mr. SCHEID. Sure.

Mrs. MILLER [continuing]. But here you have one in Columbus, New Mexico. It is up next, essentially. What is it about that particular one, that you weight economics and flow and security and all of these things, that they are up next?

Mr. SCHEID. So one of the additional considerations is prior investments that Congress has funded for a port. So with Columbus there have been several different appropriations over the past couple of years for the planning and design of the Columbus port of entry.

There are sufficient and significant needs to be addressed at that port of entry. The commercial volume there is pretty substantial. It is cyclical, but there is a significant mission need for that facility.

Congress has, on several different occasions, including——

Mrs. MILLER. In regards to the commercial, they are not even on the top 20, but continue.

Mr. SCHEID. But they have—so there are significant wait times at the Columbus port of entry, with agricultural products coming in, and there is a need to be addressed there.

In 2014 Congress appropriated $7.4 million for the design of the Columbus port of entry. It also previously received appropriations in 2009 for some design work. We believe we want to—we have got a need to be addressed and we want to continue with the construction of that project.

So having——

Mrs. MILLER. Not disputing the need.

Mr. SCHEID. Okay.

Mrs. MILLER. I mean, believe me, everybody has got a need. But if you are actually prioritizing as you have testified, this is a complete disconnect in my mind.

But at any rate, when will you be updating the list? What is your plan as far as taking a look at this 4-year-old list and taking into consideration all these various things that you have said, some that have been funded, some that have changed—various factors have changed, some that have interests in P3s, et cetera? I mean, what is your—how will you proceed on the list?

Mr. SCHEID. Coming up with a complete redo of that list in 2015, so the next fiscal year.

Mrs. MILLER. Okay. Very good. Well we certainly, obviously, are looking forward to that. I don't mean to be adversarial about this.

I know my questioning sounds that way, but I represent a community, talking about significant investment—tens of millions of dollars has been—people have lost their homes, they have been condemned, they are demolished. Businesses—I mean like auto dealerships, large businesses—condemned, demolished.

We have got 60 acres of vacant property sitting in the middle of a very busy—a city, and at the second-busiest crossing on the entire northern tier of our Nation, and, you know, and we were started at I think 87- or 86-acre plaza site, the footprint; we are now down to 16 acres. So it has significantly been—I mean, really significantly downsized, trying to work with CBP. We want to work with CBP. Obviously I use this because I happen to represent that area so I am intimately familiar with all the details of it.

But there are others—obviously, others around the country, as well. So when you look at some of these lists you think, what? The criteria just—it just doesn't make sense to me. Some of them, yes, of course; but some of them, what?

At any rate, I certainly appreciate the testimony from all the witnesses. I would say that Members of the committee may have some additional questions, as well, and we will forward those to you and ask that you would respond to those, as well.

Pursuant to the committee rule 7(e), the hearing record will be open for an additional 10 days.

I thank you very much for your attendance, again, today; particularly you, Mr. Mayor, who had to travel such a long distance. I will tell you that your Member of Congress speaks so highly not only of you but very passionately about the city that he is so honored to represent. So you have great representation here with him.

But without objection, the committee stands adjourned.

[Whereupon, at 11:37 a.m., the subcommittee was adjourned.]

APPENDIX

QUESTIONS FROM HONORABLE TOM MARINO FOR JOHN WAGNER

Question 1a. What is the process and how long does it take for GSA to begin work on a new Port of Entry compared to the time frame to enhance, expand, or improve an existing, established border operation once funding has been authorized?

Answer. GSA will respond with additional detail on this question. U.S. Customs and Border Protection (CBP) can only provide a notional timeline for a new vs. existing land port of entry (LPOE), as the lead times are port-specific and may vary based on the port's size, condition, and the amount of improvement needed to modernize the facility. Factors such as land acquisition, historic preservation, and environmental compliance can greatly affect a project's duration and must be taken into account.

Question 1b. When existing ports of entry have tangible needs and even phased renovation or enhancements under way, why wouldn't those be completed before initiating new ports of entry, especially within the same traffic corridor?

Answer. To better achieve the agency's mission, CBP, in consultation with local, State, Federal, and international partners, employs a multi-faceted planning process to assess operational needs and project opportunities. This not only includes utilizing the agency's strategic resource assessments but also factoring in regional border master planning and international infrastructure coordination, such as the U.S.-Canada Beyond the Border Initiative and U.S.-Mexico Shared Border Management Initiative.

Given a LPOE's role within a larger international transportation network, we must consider a host of inspectional and facilitation risks and opportunities when assessing investments. This includes an analysis of whether to modernize existing ports, introduce new ports, or optimize the staffing resources and technology to potentially avoid substantial capital investment altogether. In some cases, given traffic congestion and the land-locked nature of a site, the only effective long-term solution is to begin to consider investment in a new site within the transportation corridor. Furthermore, the multi-year time frame required to plan, design, and construct a selected facility, while simultaneously conducting operations, lends itself to creating an investment portfolio that phases existing LPOE investments alongside exploring opportunities for new LPOEs. Given fiscal constraints, the agency also must assess the viability of an existing port or new port project based on Federal funding availability or potential for alternative financing, in conjunction with the assessment of whether it is in the National interest.

Recognizing the dynamic and evolving mission of CBP at the border, as well as the economic/security interests of the Federal Government, international stakeholders, and border community, the agency must maintain a forward-leaning process to assess the factors outlined above and leverage a number of financial and execution tools to address existing and new port opportunities.

Question 1c. Does GSA/CBP have any obligation to complete projects that have been authorized and initiated at existing ports of entry before contemplating new ports of entry?

Answer. Although CBP does not have a specific policy that precludes the agency from engaging in new projects while simultaneously providing phased design and construction funding for existing projects, we generally do seek to follow through on projects already initiated. To address the needs of the CBP-operated portfolio of 167 LPOEs across the Southern and Northern Borders, CBP and GSA, capital construction funding permitting, typically work on multiple LPOE improvement projects in any given fiscal year, aiming to complete all such projects in an expeditious and cost-effective manner.

Question 2a. Given that Congress has authorized your agencies to begin a pilot program to use public-private partnerships to expand and improve infrastructure on the border, how can GSA/CBP better utilize these partnerships to complete and maintain current infrastructure?

Answer. Section 559 of the *Consolidated Appropriations Act, 2014,* Pub. L. 113–76 (Section 559), became law on January 17, authorizing CBP and GSA to accept donations of real property, personal property (including monetary donations) and non-personal services from private sector and Government entities. CBP and GSA may use donations accepted under Section 559 for activities associated with the construction, alteration, operations, or maintenance of new or existing ports of entry, including land acquisition, design, and the deployment of equipment and technologies.

To better leverage the partnerships established under this authority to modernize and maintain its shared port of entry portfolio, CBP and GSA are developing a criteria and procedures framework (Section 559 Framework) that, once implemented, they will use to systematically and equitably receive, evaluate, and select viable donation proposals. Moreover, the Section 559 Framework will describe the procedures that CBP, GSA, and potential donors will follow to collaboratively plan and develop selected donation proposals into executable infrastructure projects. CBP and GSA anticipate receiving a wide range of port facility improvement proposals, from equipment and technology upgrades to facility alteration and renovation projects.

Question 2b. What progress are your agencies making towards implementing policy regarding PPPs and when do your agencies expect to accept applications?

Answer. CBP and GSA are in the final stages of clearing the Section 559 Framework through an interagency review process, which will result in the document being made public as required by statute. CBP anticipates launching its new program under the Section 559 authority, to include announcing the open period for submitting donation proposals, before the end of this fiscal year.

Question 3a. How does CBP evaluate and prioritize investments in technology at ports of entry given the long time line for acquisitions approval and budget restraints of the Federal Government?

Answer. U.S. Customs and Border Protection (CBP) prioritizes investments in land port of entry (LPOE) technology as part of the overall LPOE need evaluation and prioritization process, as they compete for the same limited appropriations received from Congress despite their sometimes longer acquisition lead times. The process begins with CBP conducting Strategic Resource Assessments (SRA) to evaluate facility needs against 60 distinct criteria in four categories: Mission and Operations; Security and Life Safety; Space and Site Deficiency; and Personnel and Workload Growth. CBP employs the SRA data, which includes an architectural and analytical assessment of LPOEs along with regional planning data and studies, to determine the needs across the entire portfolio. CBP then scores facilities by criticality of need, combining the data points collected in the SRA with the criteria of the four categories.

As the next step, CBP applies two additional analyses to develop a prioritized investment, including a sensitivity analysis to determine if the results should consider factors unaccounted for through the SRA process, such as regional conditions, bilateral planning and international partner interests, or interests of other Federal, State, or local agencies.

CBP is working with DHS's Science and Technology Directorate (S&T) to implement an effective quality assurance program that measures programmatic effectiveness, and introduces process improvements to decrease errors and eliminate waste in field and headquarter operations. As this program matures, CBP will feed findings regarding technology shortfalls and how they impact programmatic effectiveness into the prioritization process.

Lastly, CBP coordinates with key stakeholders to evaluate the feasibility and risk associated with project implementation including environmental, cultural, and historic preservation requirements. CBP then arrives at a final prioritization of proposed projects and develops the capital investment plan in coordination with U.S. General Services Administration.

Question 3b. How can CBP better adapt new technologies with existing infrastructure to expedite border crossings and limit the interference with legitimate border commerce?

Answer. Leveraging technology within facility and staffing constraints to securely expedite legitimate trade and travel continues to be a CBP Office of Field Operations (OFO) priority. CBP successfully has accomplished this goal by utilizing Trusted Traveler Program processing at land and air ports of entry (POEs); Radio Frequency Identification (RFID) technology at land POEs originally implemented for Western Hemisphere Travel Initiative (WHTI) and expanded to Ready Lanes; and pedestrian reengineering to provide kiosks for travelers to swipe their own travel documents expediting the processing with the CBP Officer.

43

Business transformation is a focus of every major OFO program initiative. OFO, in coordination with the Office of Information and Technology (OIT), has created a new way of doing business called the "Project Zone" to leverage scarce resources for OFO projects and programs. The collaboration provides opportunities for OFO to continue to adapt new technologies within the existing infrastructure to expedite border crossings while facilitating legitimate trade and travel.

In order to facilitate legitimate trade and travel, CBP actively collaborates with private stakeholders to transform operations or provide solutions when required infrastructure is limited or does not exist to meet an emerging need. For example, CBP recently conducted an alternatives analysis to determine the viability of accommodating new rail service by Rocky Mountaineer from Vancouver, British Columbia to Seattle, Washington. This analysis included an assessment of appropriate operational alternatives, costs associated with those alternatives and the identification of potential operational risks. CBP deployed a mobile device solution to facilitate passenger processing leveraging wireless access the railway provided. This solution proved successful and CBP has deployed it to the maritime environment to process cruise ships where there is limited to no infrastructure in place.

Automated Passport Control (APC) is another CBP program developed through a public-private partnership, which expedites the entry process for U.S. and Canadian citizens and eligible Visa Waiver Program international travelers by providing an automated process through CBP's Primary Inspection area at participating airports. Travelers use self-service kiosks operated by a private vendor to provide responses to customs declaration questions and biographic information. APC is a free service to the traveler and does not require pre-registration or membership. Travelers using APC experience shorter wait times, less congestion, and faster processing. APC is now available in 20 international arrival airports and two preclearance airports.

CBP is currently working with S&T to evaluate the use of biometrics for exit, which ultimately we will use to facilitate the entry process. The evaluation includes how we can integrate the technology with existing facilities to increase throughput. S&T and CBP are using a test facility that mimics airport facilities so the testing will be realistic. The testing includes using test subjects to use the technology in realistic facility setting measuring the impacts of the various technologies and placement within the facility on throughput and user experience as well as the accuracy of the technology.

CBP is also working with S&T to strengthen security and trade facilitation missions by utilizing risk-based strategies, and applying a multi-layered approach to containerized cargo security. CBP's efforts in collaboration with S&T include: Developing standards to enable the use of shipper/carrier-provided data in CBP cargo targeting, as well as developing technologies and technology upgrades to improve CBP's cargo screening and cargo validation capabilities. Ultimately, these efforts will leverage existing infrastructure where possible to enhance security and improve throughput at the POEs to expedite legal commerce and travel.

Additionally, CBP is working with S&T to develop low-cost upgrades for legacy non-intrusive inspection (NII) systems as an alternative to acquiring new high performance/high maintenance machines. This effort will enable CBP to maintain robust inspection regimes while enhancing security and improving throughput at the POEs to expedite legal commerce and travel.

In order to facilitate legitimate trade, CBP is planning to expand mobile technologies for processing at the border. To better adapt new technologies, OFO and OIT have developed a proof of concept using mobile technology to provide CBP Agriculture Specialists the ability to inspect cargo and enter inspection results remotely for immediate release. The proof of concept demonstrated an immediate benefit to the trade community.

To simplify documentation for export and import, the International Trade Data System (ITDS) will establish a single portal system for the collection and distribution of trade data. Currently, some 47 Federal agencies and CBP are involved in the largely manual and paper-based trade process, which is costly and time-consuming for both the Government and the international trade community. Through the ITDS initiative, the Federal Government is creating a Single Window to transform and streamline the trade process, thereby supporting economic competitiveness. The Automated Commercial Environment (ACE) will become this Single Window—the primary system through which the international trade community submits import and export documentation that all Federal agencies require. Through ACE, Federal agencies will have more efficient automated visibility to shipment data, facilitating their import or export assessments at the border and regulating the flow of legitimate trade while also improving security, health, and safety of cargo.

44

QUESTIONS FROM HONORABLE TOM MARINO FOR MICHAEL GELBER

Question 1. What is the process and how long does it take for GSA to begin work on a new Port of Entry compared to the time frame to enhance, expand, or improve an existing, established border operation once funding has been authorized? When existing ports of entry have tangible needs and even phased renovation or enhancements under way, why wouldn't those be completed before initiating new ports of entry, especially within the same traffic corridor? Does GSA/CBP have any obligation to complete projects that have been authorized and initiated at existing ports of entry before contemplating new ports of entry?

Answer. When prioritizing new construction or major expansions at existing land ports of entry (LPOE), GSA looks to CBP's 5-year capital plan. CBP develops its 5-year plan, in coordination with GSA, using a variety of metrics, including traffic information, security issues, and detailed feasibility studies developed. At times, projects are broken into phases for a number of reasons including facilitating phased construction of a complex project that requires the continued operation of the LPOE. GSA and CBP work together to request construction funding to advance these priorities.

The construction duration of a given LPOE project depends on a wide range of factors, including the potential need to acquire a site, the scale of the project, international cooperation, and permitting issues. Generally, once a port is included in the President's budget, the time frame for project delivery is quite similar whether it is construction of a new LPOE or an expansion or improvement to an existing LPOE.

Question 2. Given that Congress has authorized your agencies to begin a pilot program to use public-private partnerships to expand and improve infrastructure on the border, how can GSA/CBP better utilize these partnerships to complete and maintain current infrastructure? What progress are your agencies making towards implementing policy regarding PPPs and when do your agencies expect to accept applications?

Answer. GSA has long-standing authority to accept unconditional gifts of property and has used this authority when State or local governments and, in a few cases, private-sector entities have elected to make donations in aid of a project or function under GSA's jurisdiction. In the case of a land port of entry (LPOE), these donations are made to realize the economic benefit that comes with a new or expanded port.

Subsection 559(f) of the Consolidated Appropriations Act of 2014, Pub. L. 113–76, broadened GSA's and CBP's gift-acceptance authority, enabling both agencies to accept donations of real or personal property (including monetary donations) and non-personal services from private sector and Government entities. Any donation accepted under this provision may be used only for necessary activities related to the construction, alteration, operation, or maintenance of a new or existing LPOE, including land acquisition, design, and the deployment of equipment and technologies.

Subsection 559(f) requires that CBP and GSA: (1) Establish criteria that identify and document their respective roles and responsibilities; (2) identify, allocate, and manage potential risk; (3) define clear, measurable objectives; and (4) publish criteria for evaluating partnership projects.

Since the enactment of the legislation, CBP and GSA have coordinated closely to satisfy this statutory requirement and jointly developed the *Section 559 Donation Acceptance Authority Proposal Evaluation Procedures & Criteria Framework (559 Framework).* This document outlines the procedures and criteria that CBP and GSA will use systematically and equitably to receive, evaluate, select, plan, develop, and formally accept proposed donations under subsection 559(f). These proposals may come from private corporations, public entities, municipalities, port authorities, consortiums, and any other private-sector or Government entities interested in donating real property, personal property, or non-personal services.

The *559 Framework* has been released and posted on both CBP and GSA websites to coincide with a program launch announcement that will include proposal submission procedures. The 559 Framework is available to all potential donors and will enable CPB and GSA to evaluate the operational and nonoperational merit of each proposal, based on the published evaluation criteria.

Question 3a. How does CBP evaluate and prioritize investments in technology at ports of entry given the long time line for acquisitions approval and budget restraints of the Federal Government?

Question 3b. How can CBP better adapt new technologies with existing infrastructure to expedite border crossings and limit the interference with legitimate border commerce?

Answer. Question No. 3 is for CBP, not GSA.

○

www.ingramcontent.com/pod-product-compliance
Lightning Source LLC
Chambersburg PA
CBHW080619290526
45790CB00007B/2845